OUR LAND AND OUR LADY

OUR LAND AND OUR LADY

By DANIEL SARGENT

"O admirabile commercium"

LONGMANS, GREEN AND CO.

NEW YORK · TORONTO

LONGMANS, GREEN AND CO., INC.
55 FIFTH AVENUE, NEW YORK 3

LONGMANS, GREEN AND CO. LTD.
39 PATERNOSTER ROW, LONDON, E.C. 4
17 CHITTARANJAN AVENUE, CALCUTTA
NICOL ROAD, BOMBAY
36A MOUNT ROAD, MADRAS

LONGMANS, GREEN AND CO.
215 VICTORIA STREET, TORONTO 1

OUR LAND AND OUR LADY

First Edition September 1939
Reprinted December 1939
January 1940, May 1941
March 1943, May 1946

PRINTED IN THE UNITED STATES OF AMERICA

CONTENTS

v

4113

OUR LAND AND OUR LADY

Our Land and Our Lady

CHAPTER I

THE *SANTA MARIA*

IN OUR beginning it was the *Santa Maria* that sailed toward our shores — Columbus's *Santa Maria*, Queen Isabella's *Santa Maria*, Castile's *Santa Maria*, Christendom's *Santa Maria*. She never reached our shores, for on October 12, 1492, she came to the island which we call Watling's and which Columbus christened San Salvador ; and round it she turned as round a traffic-signal, and steered first south and at last southeast, and ended up impaled on a rock on Christmas Day off the north coast of Haiti. She never reached our shores. But she had been pointing to them. She had been Florida-bound. She has left a furrow in the ocean that pointed to them as an arrow points to its mark.

That furrow never closed. Because it never closed, it became, for our country and for the entire New World, history's most important furrow. Other ships, Norse, English, Irish, Breton, Basque or Portuguese may have come to our land from Europe before the *Santa Maria* made its incomplete voyage to our Florida, but their furrows closed, disappeared. They made no bridge. The *Santa Maria*, on the other hand, connected the New World forever with the Old. She brought Europe's affair — the affair of the centuries, as Saint Bernard called it — the Incarnation, Christ born of the Virgin Mary, to the New World. From then on the New World was drawn into a drama from which she could never free herself. There had indeed been a drama in the New World before the arrival to it of the *Santa Maria*, a drama of people, like ourselves, Adam-descended, and, like us, trying to build immortal cities. But after the furrow had been made by the *Santa Maria*, the terms of that drama were different, its quarrels were different, its heroisms were different. It is not recorded that any land which has heard of the Incarnation has been able wholly to forget it, not even though it detest the Incarnation as Satan detested the sun. The *Santa Maria* brought the Incarnation to the New World. It made for all of those in the New World the furrow of furrows.

It also gave us our Discoverer. A discoverer is a most tenuous thing to give to a land, almost an invisible thing, for a discoverer leaves not even a foot-print. He comes. He is gone. Yet a discoverer haunts a land. Our human minds, source-seeking, look back to him. As a savage tribe believes itself to be guarded, accompanied forever, or threatened, by its first ancestor — a ghost ever in its midst — so we are accompanied by our land's discoverer. We turn and he is there. He may be as immaterial as the air, but he is so immaterial that he cannot be erased. He is like a thought with which we think.

So the *Santa Maria* gave us something momentous in giving us a discoverer, and it so happened that the discoverer she gave us was momentous in himself. Particularly for us in the United States was he momentous, for we of all nations in the world are recorded as the most avid in the pursuit of wealth, and yet we are credulously romantic and idealistic. We want wealth not cynically, but for some cause, we know not what. Columbus knew well his cause ; he wished the world's gold in order to use it to free Jerusalem from the Turk, and in order indirectly to convert the world. But he presents well the paradox that our country presents. He was humble and died accoutered in the robe of the Third Order of St. Francis, yet he refused to make the voyage across the ocean unless he were promised honors that would make him almost a king. He endangered even his chances of immortal fame in this world by stickling for a title that would not last. Strange discoverer ! Yet how appropriate for a fantastically strange land ! The most paradoxical land that Christendom has yet produced looks to a discoverer who presents ever for its thoughts the complete human paradox, and, more significant, the complete human Christian paradox.

The *Santa Maria* also gave us an owner : Spain. All of us acknowledge Columbus as our discoverer, but few of us ever think of Spain as our first owner. She was our first owner. She was Plymouth Rock's first owner. She owned, because of the *Santa Maria's* furrow, all of our land for a half-century without dispute. She owned all of it, though with some dispute, for one hundred years. During nearly two hundred years she owned nine-tenths of it. For three hundred and fifty years up till 1847, she (and her successor, Mexico) continued to own a third of it.

To have been owned for so long a time by Spain is something that made a difference to us, for Spain is a land not without peculiarity. She is separated from the other nations of Christendom by more than the Pyrenees. Some people would try to characterize her strangeness by saying that she is less capable of change than her neighbors, and surely many a good thing, and no doubt some bad things, have persevered in the Iberian Peninsula long after they have disappeared elsewhere. Don Quixote could be written about there, in the sixteenth century, because there he lived, whereas in France and England he had long since died. But it would be laughable to describe Spain as the land which could not change, for what could we do with the fact that Castile, which did not know the tiller from the prow of a boat before Columbus's time, became after his voyage the mistress of the seas. Spain is not changeless, she is not the past. One might well call her the future, for she lived as an Empire experiences which England is only facing now. Spain has her peculiarities but they are not changelessness.

Is it not best to characterize Spain simply as the country that has no sense of time and space ? She fought the Moors for eight hundred years and she scarcely noticed it. In the sixteenth century she found half the earth fallen her heritage and she was barely awed. She has so little sense of the height of heaven from earth that she treats the saints in glory as if they were in immediate proximity to her living, breathing citizens not in glory. She has such an ardor of love that without irreverence she can let the sons of her soil be christened Jesús. We were presented by the *Santa Maria* to a country which even in heaven seems to have attracted notice ; she was given the portentous lot of sending forth the *Santa Maria*.

We were presented to an owner so singularly tied to eternity, that she has the Christian abandonment of sleep, and also, the Christian power of resurrection.

But not only was Spain a very special owner, she was an owner given unheard-of responsibilities. When Alexander VI, acting as mediator between the two exploring countries, Spain and Portugal, drew the line which gave the Americas (all save Brazil) to Spain, when he performed this act, which many have thought so arrogant, he made various stipulations which those who complain of his lordliness, are apt to forget. Neither Spain nor Portugal was recognized as having an unconditional ownership of the newly discovered lands. They were obliged to bring the Christian faith to the inhabitants of those lands, or to do their best so to do ; otherwise their ownership was forfeit. They were to treat the peoples they pacified with Christian charity and they were to preach the good news of Christian Revelation to them ; in other words, they were to be apostles. That this obligation might be more easily complied with, the rulers of the two countries received special and unprecedented privileges. They were allowed to keep the ecclesiastical tithes collected in the new regions, not for themselves but for the expense of providing the necessary missionaries, and for building the churches and missions. Also they were entrusted with the naming of the bishops.

When Spain came first to be our owner, she was the one country in Europe endowed with the shadow of omnipotence. She alone could think of being able to do what she wanted to do. She was receiving the gold from America of which Columbus had dreamed. She had an army which was so invincible in Europe that it remained invincible for a century and a half. She had talent, energy, confidence, unity. Even with all of this omnipotence, however, she could not be everywhere. She devoted her omnipotence more to Central and South America and to Mexico than to the region of our forty-eight states. And she did this deliberately, because her explorer, Gómez, in 1524 had sailed along our entire Atlantic seaboard and told Spain that our country was sadly commonplace — no better than Europe. Yet even then Spain did not utterly neglect a land so stigmatized. Detachments of her soldiery, representing their country's courage and enterprise and grandeur of ambition, made forays into our territory that remain as an astounding legend. Our whole southland would acquire a shallowness if Coronado's and De Soto's magnificent marches were taken away from them. It adds a depth and plenitude to the flatness of the State of Kansas when in its fields is picked up, as it was in 1886, a sword which had been dropped there in 1540; on it was written the name Juan Gallegos, with the inscription on the blade: "Do not draw me without right. Do not sheathe me without honor."

Then Spain lost her omnipotence, but she did not turn her back entirely on our land. She ceased her grandiose, vague forays, but with prudence and perseverance she occupied various portions of it. If we are asked if those occupations were of any moment, we have only to counter-ask if it would be of any moment were there no Spanish mission-churches in California, nor in Arizona, and New Mexico, and no Spanish ruins in Texas. Merely as the creator of what we see as ruins, they, the Spaniards, accomplished something. Were there no such ruins, we should not be brought up short in our commercial pride and short-sightedness. We should never now have the privilege of gasping : "What was this great generosity, this other worldliness which left here its traces ?"

But also Spanish ownership was important for its effect on English colonial history, and on our American history. Had England not come to our shores as a surreptitious squatter, and not at all as a confident owner, she would never have chosen to settle at such northerly and penurious ports. She would have gone to the Gulf of Mexico to the south, believing — as all the world believed — that what was paradisiacal and gold-ore-bearing was the land nearest the equator. Had it not been for Spanish ownership, England would never have had the sense to occupy the lands which were, in the end, best for her to occupy, lands calculated to discipline the settlers that colonized them and to keep them concentrated and stable, thus forcing upon them a domesticity of life which was all for England's good.

Finally, let us not forget that Spanish ownership of the United States continued to have an effect on those English colonists after they ceased to be colonists and had become Americans of the United States. Spain, to begin with, helped us to our independence. The Spanish expeditions from New Orleans which captured Natchez from the English and Florida during our Revolution, were not at all minor affairs in numbers or in heroism. Spain was still alive. She was so alive that she sent an expedition even from St. Louis (Missouri) to Lake Michigan to capture the English fort at St. Joseph. And she was still so alive in Louisiana after our independence had been gained that she continued for a generation as our rival. She took for a time our hero, Daniel Boone, from us, employing him as her Spanish magistrate for ten years in Spanish Arkansas. And after the Louisiana purchase, after Arkansas was no longer Spanish Arkansas, and after Missouri was ours, and the Missouri River, it was the existence of still a remaining part of the Spanish-owned United States that sent our caravans first to the west. Had there been no Santa Fé, New Mexico, had there been but a desert there, or a few Indian pueblos, the ox-carts would never have crossed the plains. The western expansion would have had to wait.

The ship, the *Santa Maria*, which had such an effect on our destiny, was a ship which wore with reason her name. She came from a Europe which had preserved her youth and joyfulness through confidence in the unique human being after whom the *Santa Maria* was named — Saint Mary, Our Lady. She came from a part of Europe, Spain — the Spain of Our Lady of the Pillar of Saragossa — which at that time was Our Lady's, Santa Maria's, special champion. She had sailed from Europe and from Spain at a period of history when sailormen of Christendom — hers among them — still sang every evening the "Salve Regina," and still told the time of day as being before or after that Salve Regina hour. And Columbus, its commander, was so much Our Lady's, that he wove her initials into his signature, and carefully prescribed that he should be buried in her chapel dedicated to the Immaculate Conception, in the valley known as the Conception in Haiti.

It is impossible to begin to think about the history of our country without thinking of the *Santa Maria*. The *Santa Maria* stands like the frontispiece in the book of all our deeds. She is the illuminated capital, brilliant, awakening, at the beginning of our chronicle of record. He who does not see that ship leaves the book still closed, and drowses and dozes, and puts off till tomorrow his reading.

CHAPTER II

THE SPANISH EXPLORERS

IT WAS NOT until twenty years after the *Santa Maria* had sunk that a ship continued the *Santa Maria*'s furrow from the island of San Salvador to the coast of the United States. On April 2nd, 1512, Juan Ponce of the ancient Spanish kingdom of León took the first look at our country. The day was Palm Sunday and on Palm Sunday in old Spanish liturgical custom Easter was already said to be in flower — *Pascua* was said to be *Florida* — and therefore Juan Ponce de León called the land which he came on (somewhere near our Palm Beach), Florida. Our country began by being called a land in flower.

The man who gave our country its first name is often described and pictured in our country's school-books as a visionary youth who, tricked up in hat-plumes and velvet capes, was seeking the fountain of perpetual youth. Had he been really young, he would have thought that he did not need the fountain of youth. As it was, he was in his weather-worn forties and too old and too experienced to be credulous in such things. He came to Florida simply because he wanted to be as independent as possible.

He had begun to make his way in life by fighting as a foot-soldier in the Christian armies of Queen Isabella that took Granada from the Moors in 1492. After that he was a crusader without a crusade, and in 1493 he enlisted as one of the fifteen hundred young individualists who joined Columbus on his second, enthusiastic, over-confident voyage to the New World.

In the New World, on the island of Haiti, he became an *encomandero*. That is, he was one of those lordlings, set over a piece of land and a group of Indians, who were to be responsible not only for ruling those Indians but for making Christians out of them. Thus he had the obligation given to him that Alexander VI had given to Ferdinand and Isabella. He was a little king, but even then not independent enough.

He went, therefore, at his own expense to the island of Puerto Rico, and pacified it for Spain and for Christendom on his own account. He was appointed by the King its first governor. He might then have been happy had not the Viceroy of the Indies, Columbus' son Diego, claimed and won jurisdiction over him. Annoyed at this, he obtained permission from King Ferdinand to sail northwest and pacify a new land in that direction over which he could be governor unhampered by a viceroy.

He found the new land, gave it its name, Florida, and reconnoitered it preparatory to doing what he liked to do most — rule it. But colonizing Florida would cost money. It was not till eight years later that he could write a letter to his new sovereign, Charles V : "Among my services I discovered at my own cost and charge, the Island of Florida and others in its district, which are not mentioned as being small and useless ; and I now return to that island, if it please God's will, to settle it, being enabled to carry a number of people with whom I shall be able to do so, that the name of Christ may be praised there, and Your Majesty served with the fruit that land produces. I shall set out to pursue my voyage hence in five or six days."

Ponce de León did return to that island (as he called it) but he did not settle it, and he did not rule it, for he was shot by an Indian arrow at Charlotte Harbor on Florida's west coast, and he died of the wound as he sailed back to Cuba.

He was on paper the first governor of the United States, for he was appointed Governor of Florida, and Florida was the whole of our country. Yet quite rightly no one remembers him as such. Instead he is remembered as the first of the Spanish explorers of our land, the first of the explorers of that nation which did more than any other country to reveal what was the shape of our country, and what was its character, and what were the beasts and the trees within it, and what were the men. It was the Spaniards who charted first both our Atlantic and our Pacific coasts by sailing along them. They disclosed the secrets of its entire southern half by making their pioneer pathways through it. For a hundred years after Ponce de León Spain was the only country which knew anything about our land. She had a monopoly of geographic information concerning our future states, and tried even to keep it her monopoly. The other countries — France and England — learned what they did about our land by stealing information through diplomatic channels, or by buying information from renegades.

When La Salle tried to found his colony at the end of the seventeenth century near the Mississippi's mouth (and founded it by mistake in Texas), he was guided by directions received by him from the Spanish renegade ex-governor of New Mexico, Peñalosa. Still later, when President Jefferson, who had made the Louisiana Purchase, wished to send Lewis and Clark exploring into the new acquisition, he still relied on Spanish geographical knowledge and supplied them with reports of a Spanish exploring company of the late eighteenth century : the "Compañia de Descubridores del Missouri."

Ponce de León even on his first voyage had made valuable discoveries. He had learned that Florida was shaped like a thumb for he had sailed on both sides of it. He had also discovered the best way out of the Gulf of Mexico toward Europe : the Bahama Channel, the dark streak of water along Florida's east coast where the white disagreeable shoals do not show through. And before Ponce's death, Piñeda had explored the arc of the Gulf of Mexico's shore from Vera Cruz to Florida's tip ; he had even noticed the Mississippi's mouth, and called that river the Espiritú Santo. And hardly had Ponce died of his arrow wound than Gómez, a Portuguese in Spanish employ, had explored the Atlantic coast from Florida's tip to Labrador.

But these were but maritime adventures. The first to test once again our land, as Ponce had tried to do, was his first real successor, Lucas Vásquez de Ayllón. The latter was not nearly the soldier that Ponce was, but his career in the New World rhymes with that of his predecessor. Like Ponce he was a government official, in his case of Haiti. Like Ponce he fitted out an expedition at his own expense. And he had a similar goal : he wished to be lord somewhere of all he surveyed. He sailed from Haiti in July 1526 with six ships and six hundred colonists, bound for our Virginia.

With him he took also a man who was more important than all the six hundred colonists, and much better known than he : Father Montesinos, a Dominican friar. We have all heard of Bishop Bartolomé de Las Casas, the fiery defender of oppressed Indians, but we have not all heard of Friar Montesinos, who awakened Las Casas, and who was a wiser man than he, and a much better missionary. Twenty-five years before he had begun to rebuke the *encomanderos* of Haiti for their cruel treatment of the natives. He had incurred their wrath, but not the wrath of the King. He had received royal favor. He had secured new royal laws from King Ferdinand for the protection of the Indians. Whether he had been forced on Ayllón we do not know. At any rate he went with him, and was well treated by him. He was Ayllón's conscience, and a reminder to him of his obligation to convert the Indians.

But Ayllón neither established a kingdom for himself, nor converted the Indians. The expedition started well. It came to the most important bay on our eastern coast, Chesapeake Bay — the estuary that points like an arrowhead toward our capital city, Washington — and gave to it the name of the Bay of the Mother of God. There a landing was made at what is generally conceded to be the site of the future English colony at Jamestown, Virginia. The arrival was on Saint Michael's Day and the new colony received the name San Miguel de Gualdape. Eighty-one years before the English first arrived at that site, Friar Montesinos, the apostle who made an apostle to the Indians out of Bartolomé de Las Casas, celebrated the first Mass on Virginia's soil. The chapel in which he celebrated it is, so far as we know, the first chapel ever built on the territory of the United States. But there the good luck ended. A pestilence broke out that killed three hundred of the colonists. Ayllón himself died of it, and the expedition sailed back to San Domingo, Friar Montesinos still with it.

So far the United States had been treated by the Spaniards as if it were a long, low, inconvenient island which separated them from what we call the Pacific and which they called the South Sea. Its interior did not attract them. Both Ponce de León and Lucas Vásquez de Ayllón had rather assumed that it had none, but they were so little explorers in spirit that they asked themselves few questions about it. It was an even more unwilling explorer than they, however, who turned Spain's attention to our interior, and who himself in most incongruous garb — stark nakedness — penetrated it and crossed it. His name was the incongruous name Cabeza de Vaca — or in English, Cow's Head.

That he should have gloried in this name throws a light upon him and upon many other thousand Spaniards. Three hundred years before he was born, a Spanish Christian shepherd had brought victory to the Spanish Christian armies in July 1212, at Las Navas de Tolosa, in their battle against the unchristian Moors, by marking a mountain pass with cows' heads to guide the Christian army to unexpected victory. Our Cabeza de Vaca was through his mother descended from this illustrious shepherd, and though he was through his father descended from the wealthy and noble conquerors of the Canary Islands, the de Veras, he was much prouder of his shepherd than of his conquistador ancestry. He was Cabeza de Vaca, and while still proud to be Cabeza de Vaca, and because he was a soldierly Cabeza de Vaca, he joined the soldierly expedition of Pánfilo de Narváez which went to the northern shores of the Gulf of Mexico to pacify that region in the name of Spain. Pánfilo de Narváez was to be governor of the entire curve of our country from Pánuco in Mexico, to Key West in Florida, that is of Texas, Louisiana, Mississippi, Alabama and part of Florida. Cabeza de Vaca was to be his high-sheriff and treasurer.

Within a year of his arrival under Narváez in West Florida, Cabeza de Vaca found himself one of the half-dozen survivors of the original five hundred of that expedition. Narváez had wandered first in circles in the forests. He had discovered that in swamps thick with trees and treacherous with quags and hummocks it was not easy to play the part of a cavalry-leading Cortez. He had therefore slaughtered his horses, made bellows of their hides, and with the strange forges thus contrived had built a fleet of undecked boats in which to sail back to Mexico. Then the storm had struck the boats, and the waves had broken over them, and they could not steer. Cabeza de Vaca had been lucky enough to be washed ashore on an island which he called unlucky, Malhado, and which is usually supposed to have been near Galveston, Texas. He was not unprepared for hardships. He had expected there would be fighting. But he found himself at Galveston beginning a new life as a starving slave to starving Indians. This was more than he had ever bargained for.

In order to be able to penetrate and cross our country, it seemed as if a white man had first to humble himself and become an Indian. Cabeza de Vaca did humble himself. For seven years he was an Indian slave. He accepted this hardship as a penance.

"In these labors," he said, "my only solace and relief were in thinking of Our Redeemer, Jesus Christ, and in the blood He shed for me, in considering how much greater must have been the torment He sustained from the thorns than that I received." On his first arrival in Texas, after the shipwreck, he had been naked. Now his nakedness had become his uniform, for the Indians dressed him like themselves and being the poorest and most naked of Indians, they gave him for his costume a cincture. Finally when he even began to look like an Indian, he escaped westward with three companians — Maldonado, Dorantes, and Estevanico, an Arabian Black. Texas, through which he and the three were making their way, was a part of our country occupied in the old days by the most diverse tribes of Indians, different in race, language and civilization one from another and constantly warring. It was not easy to preserve one's life in a trek across Texas, but Cabeza de Vaca accomplished it by accepting an honor that was forced upon him, by the Indians, one and all. He was regarded by them as a healer. The honor filled him with some awesomeness. He was too noble to practise trickery, too Christian to pretend to divine attributes. When the sick were brought to him he practised on them White Man's medicine when it was possible. Simply by intelligence and manual dexterity he accomplished various feats of surgery, such as the extracting of arrow-heads. When the Indians in other cases begged him to perform cures simply by the laying-on of hands, he trembled and then prayed over them, repeating the far-away Christian prayers of his Christian Spain. Some of the cures, real or imagined, were so extraordinary that he was further humbled by his own success. As he trod west with the sun rising daily behind him, he became more and more to the eyes of the Indians "the child of the Sun."

He was an explorer who had both time in which to observe, and keen eyes with which to see. He crossed Texas and came to adobe houses two stories high. He saw a turquoise or two. But the Indians fascinated him more than the turquoises. In his misery he could not feel aloof from them. He regarded them with sympathy, and was particularly touched by one tribe of Indians who seemed to be exceptional to the others, and who were to prove really exceptional to the others in their readiness to accept Christ's law: the Jumanos. Their manner of greeting him touched his heart. They did not come forth to meet him: their reverence was profound but unexpected; they stayed in their houses.

"They were seated with their faces turned to the wall, their heads down, their hair brought before their eyes [these are de Vaca's own words] and their property placed in a heap in the middle of the house. From this place they began to give us many blankets of skin; they had nothing they did not bestow."

Cabeza de Vaca came to northwest Texas where the

Pecos River flows into the Rio Grande, and then crossing the Rio Grande proceeded southwesterly till he came to the settlements of New Spain. He was safe at last. But he could not sleep, not in a bed, and the feeling of clothes on his skin was an irritation worse than vermin. For ten years he had been an Indian. He was still so much at one with them, that his wrath was bitter when the outlaw band of Spanish frontiersmen tried to enslave his escort. He appealed to the King's officers and saved them from that fate.

Cabeza de Vaca had given dimension to our country. It was not merely a long sand-spit. From Galveston to the corner of New Mexico, which he had neared, was six hundred miles. It began to take shape to the Spaniards. They knew its Atlantic coastline. They knew that it had a thousand miles of width. Only in regard to its extent to the northwest were they at fault. They thought the Gulf of California opened into an inland sea, that California was but an island, that Oregon, Idaho, Montana, Nevada and Wyoming were under water, that beyond that water was Tartary, that between Tartary and northern Colorado were the straits of Anian through which there was a passage from the Atlantic to the Pacific.

Cabeza de Vaca, however, did more than add to geographic knowledge. He was involuntarily the great instigator of further exploration. Had he not mentioned turquoises? Had he not confessed to have seen two-story houses? Because he was like a man raised from the dead, all that he said, even the most prosaically, was considered as marvellous. It was deemed that he had caught sight of the Seven Cities of ancient far eastern legend. Compared to what he had seen, the Mexico of Cortez was nothing.

Immediately there set forth three expeditions for the Seven Cities : Cabrillo's a maritime expedition from the Pacific coast of New Spain or Mexio ; and De Soto's starting from Florida ; and Coronado's marching from Campostela in Mexico northward overland. All of these expeditions had one goal : Cabrillo hoped to come to the Seven Cities by rounding California Island's northern tip and continuing east through the Straits of Anian. De Soto would begin where Narváez had — so it was thought — lost his nerve. Coronado would proceed directly to the region where Cabeza de Vaca had seen the turquoises and been so little interested in them.

Cabrillo made the shortest voyage in point of time, though he — or rather his ships — were away for nine months. He sailed from Acapulco in southwest Mexico in three ships that were all of them Pacific-built, and showed it. Only one of them was decked. It was a full ocean trip for him to come even to the tip of Lower California — one thousand miles.

Lower California, the peninsula, is another seven hundred miles. Before Cabrillo arrived at our California, he had sailed with ill-supplied ships nearly two thousand miles. It was time already to turn back. Then he himself died from stumbling on California's shore. That was double reason for turning back. Yet the master-pilot took charge and on they went. Just how far they persevered we do not quite know — to Oregon it is said. At any rate they stayed away nine months even though they made some fast time on a hurricane south. In their return they were so scurvy-riddled that they could not possibly have gone all the way to Acapulco. The two remaining ships had to land farther up on the Mexican coast to give the crews a chance to crawl ashore, gnaw some roots and end their scurvy.

Of all the expeditions Cabrillo's had the poorest luck in regard to finding any Seven Cities. It saw the watch-fires of Lower California's Indians, and no other habitations of man. But the geographic information it brought back defined our Pacific coast as the Atlantic coast had already been defined. The entrance to the Straits of Anian must be north of southern Oregon. Our country was growing to its real dimensions.

De Soto's expedition was like a military foray from Spain, such as might, in the old days a generation back, have proceeded against the Moors in Spain. It sailed from Spain and was filled with young Spanish hidalgoes. There were six hundred men in the expedition, of whom three hundred were mounted.

Unfortunately for De Soto, the land of Florida, which he entered at Tampa, was not the firm cavalry country of Spain, nor that of Moorish northern Africa. It was swamps and tangled forests, with no hills from which one could survey the surrounding terrain. Marching through it was like marching blindfold. And how could the horses be fed? And how find supplies for six hundred men? And the Indians did not fight in battle-array.

De Soto met only one piece of good luck; he discovered in Florida's forests a Spaniard, named Ortiz, who had been lost from the expedition of Narváez and was living as a slave to the Indians. Ortiz could act as interpreter. Perhaps without Ortiz he would have turned back. But with Ortiz there was hope, for Ortiz could receive information and misinformation from the Indians.

There was no use staying in Florida. There were no Seven Cities there, but through Ortiz he learned of villages, possibly cities to the northeast.

De Soto started across Georgia and South Carolina for North Carolina, as if bent on reaching the Bay of the Mother of God, or on capturing the City of Washington that did not exist. On his way he had more than one good meal on Indian corn, and he found not only hostile Indians but friendly ones, but no cities.

Then he swerved west. No cities in the Alleghanies. No cities in North Carolina, in Tennessee, in Alabama, in Mississippi. Only stockades to be fought against.

At the end of a year De Soto had the chance to sail home, for ships were in the offing. It was the advisable thing to do. The armor of his soldiers was still armor, though in rust, but their clothing had turned to tatters, and the tatters could only be replaced with woven straw. Their appearance of glory had gone, and their puissance was reduced ; one-half of the men were dead, and two-thirds of the horses. And the hostile Indians were ever more formidable. They had arrows which in their splintering could go through chain armor. He still had Indian allies but they were weary of his alliance, and wondered what it profited them to give the Spaniards their maize. Harder and harder it was to find among them those who would become a part of the Spanish baggage train and carry their baggage.

Yet De Soto chose to disregard the ships, to go on once more. It had taken eight hundred years to reconquer Spain and there was still time to go on to Arkansas and Texas. And he did go on and he came to the Mississippi River. It was broad as a strait a mile wide, and it flowed — an impressive military barrier. Yet cross it he would, and did, building light barges for the transport. He accomplished the feat even in the face of a watchful foe. He saw his army march into Arkansas and Louisiana and Texas. He saw it in the open plains, saw it staring at the buffalo, saw it in the Ozark hills, saw it finally again on the muddy, over-flowed shores of the immense Mississippi. But then he saw it no more. He died.

Yet even with his death the campaign could not end. Its marchings continued, as indeed they had to ; a way home had to be found. Finally the marching ceased. There was but one way of home-return. A ship-yard was improvised on the banks of the Mississippi near the mouth of the Red River and seven brigantines were built which finally slid down the current toward the gulf. For four years these soldiers, who had not lost their morale, had lived citizens of the United States. Four years is a long time.

There had been with the expedition originally one white woman, an officer's wife. Before a year had passed she was with child, and it was while with child that she was killed by the Indians. Had the babe been born, it might have grown up and begun to speak Spanish without ever having seen anything but soldiers, camps, forests ; Arkansas, Texas, Louisiana. Four years would have been an eternity to the child. It was a long time even for grown men. When they arrived at Pánuco, Mexico, they did not have to be very religious to want first — first even before feasting — to be present at a Mass of Thanksgiving for their escape.

As a military foray which lasted for four years and never got in sight of its objective, and which never even discovered what its objective was, De Soto's expedition was unique. But it was equally unique as an exploring success. It brought back a map of the shores of the Gulf of Mexico on which the rivers were marked as straight lines like the cracks between keys on the piano-board, but the line of the coast was true, and the rivers were all there, and if they were plotted too straight it was simply because they seemed always to come straight across the line of March like an enemy's moats — most painfully so. Much more important than their black-and-white map was the information they brought back. They had slept in the valleys, the hills, the plains, even the swamps of our southland and had known them in pain and hardship, and in every season. They had become native to some ten of our States. They had learned what animals we had, how tasty were possums, how easy it was to starve on squirrels, what a feast was the buffalo of the plains. De Soto had discovered our southern States as one who lives and dies in a country discovers it by becoming a part of it.

The expedition of Coronado was better advised. He who planned it was the greatest of all New Spain's viceroys — Mendoza — a man firm enough of hand to enforce obedience, tender enough of conscience to want to follow wholly the policy toward the Indians advocated by Las Casas. Before he despatched Coronado to the Seven Cities, he sent first a friar, Marco of Nice, to see if they really existed. Friar Marco, taking one of Cabeza de Vaca's companions with him, came to southwest New Mexico, saw the pueblos, houses piled on houses, the chimneys smoking, the watchers on the battlements. And he saw cliffs and mesas, sculptured mountains in the distance, which looked like not seven but a thousand cities, and he came back with news : there was indeed a promised land to the north.

Mendoza did not send forth a mere military foray for conquest but rather a Spanish city which was simply to move in among the other cities, already on paper Spain's, and there introduce the King of Spain's protection. This city was composed first of three hundred Spaniards, who were men of energy, fitted for a fearless frontier, but somewhat too unruly for the New Spain into which he was putting order. Then the city, ambulatory toward the north, was composed of fifteen hundred Indian allies. And it moved with its own market-place, one thousand horses, five thousand rams and ewes. At its head, for its governor, was Coronado. With it went half a dozen Franciscans, to preach to the cities, to keep the Christian life alive amid Coronado's men. Leading the Franciscans was Friar Marco. Coronado led his city up the west coast of Mexico, or New Spain, came to the Zuñi pueblos, and then swerved east, coming to the Rio Grande River, which, because it was

first seen on Our Lady's birthday, September 8th, received and held for a short time the title of Our Lady's River. He thought of planting his city in the valley of the Rio Grande, but it was very cold there in this beginning winter. And he was disappointed in the pueblos he had found. Also there had been a quarrel with the Indians, for never has there been an occupying army that did not give offense. There was one other reason for not establishing his city in the Rio Grande Valley. There were plenty of these mud cities which looked as if they had gold, but not a one that possessed any.

Coronado sent forth various expeditions to discover better cities where there was gold. One expedition under Cardeñas came to a great red gully a mile deep, the Grand Cañon of the Colorado River ; another marching east came to plains that seemed to move — the migratory buffalo herds interminable — but there was no gold. Finally he himself rode with thirty men and several friars to a place where a strange Indian, whom the Spaniards called Turco, and who had come from the direction of the Gulf of Mexico, said there was limitless gold. The place was called Quivira. It was to the northeast. When Coronado arrived there, he found some straw huts, nothing more. The place was a plain, probably a part of flat Kansas, probably Wichita, Kansas. The disappointment was great, yet Coronado preferred the climate and the soil's fertility to New Mexico. He planned to move his city from the Rio Grande to Kansas. He planned to found Wichita.

Yet the plan fell through. One of his chroniclers says that he was a softy and wished to be home to his wife in

New Spain. He had been nevertheless an able and brave and very canny captain. The cause of his return was, first, that not even in Kansas were there any Seven Cities, and, second, that his men were growing mutinous at not having found them. So back he went to Mexico.

He too brought back more than a failure. He brought back a map, and he brought back an official description of the countries traversed, which Mendoza had ordered him to make, but which is now lost. Also he brought back a great deal of information, some of it written, some of it very accurate, some of it extraordinarily picturesque. Castañeda's portrait of the buffalo is a masterpiece :

"They have a narrow, short face, the brow two palms across from eye to eye, the eye is sticking out at the side, so that when they are running they can see who is following them. They have very long beards, like goats, and when they are running they throw back their heads with the beard dragging on the ground. In May they change the hair in the middle of the body for a down, which makes perfect lions of them. They have a short tail with a bunch of hair at the end. When they run, they carry it erect like a scorpion."

Coronado and his men had discovered what our Arizona is like, and our New Mexico, and Oklahoma, and Texas, and Kansas. He brought to light the nature of our entire southwest : the strangeness of its sculptured mountains, the rich monotony of the unending plains of Kansas.

After this effervescence of Spanish exploration, there came a slowing down. There were various reasons for the lull. First, Coronado's report of the winds and snows of New Mexico was a deterrent. Second, silver mines had been discovered in northern New Spain, and why go farther north? But most of all, royal ordinances ferociously forbade further irresponsible exploration. It was too costly. It caused trouble.

But missionaries were not considered irresponsible explorers. They did not attack the Indians, and caused therefore no Indian reprisals. Moreover, they were entitled to their apostolic freedom, and the king did not interfere with it. He counted all missionaries as authorized explorers. Of course their expeditions had to cost some money, and it was hard therefore to start forth on them without some kind of official aid. Yet some missionaries, even on their own initiative, did an extraordinary amount of exploration. One of these was the mathematical missionary, Father Kino, the Tyrolean Jesuit, who in the last years of the seventeenth century spent his life on horse-back far to the northwest of New Spain, investigating with a geographer's accuracy Arizona and the mouth of the Colorado River, making in all, says his biographer Bolton, forty expeditions, some of them eight hundred miles in extent.

There were other authorized explorers, those whom the king sent forth for a specific purpose. Such was Vizcaino, who in 1599 discovered Monterey Bay, California, while looking for a good port of shelter and repair for the Philippine galleons. Such was another de León, no relation to Juan Ponce who, a hundred years later, explored Texas in order to keep out La Salle and the French. Such was Villasur who, in 1726, died on the

South Platte River in Nebraska, having gone there also
to ward off the French, and having probably with French
connivance been ambushed and killed by the Pawnees.
Such were Portalá and Anza and Friar Junípero Serra
who in the late eighteenth century were sent to California to keep out the Russians.

In the end the Spanish explorers came to be of a New
World type. The type had three varieties: the Spanish trader of the Mississippi Valley during the days
when New Orleans and St. Louis were Spanish; the
Spanish "leather-jackets" of the Southwest; and the
Franciscans from Mexico. Of these varieties the first
was least important, for the Spanish as traders never
equalled the French, nor the English. And one of the
best Spanish exploring traders had a suspiciously Scotch
name, Mackay. The second was very important. And
the third even more so.

The "leather-jackets," or the second type, were so
called because they wore a leather fold flung over the
shoulders, which could be used as armor against arrows.
They were Indian fighters brought up in border warfare, who could imitate the ways of the Indians, and who
on some occasions disguised themselves as Comanches
in order to fight Comanches. Anza, the greatest of
them all, became military governor of New Mexico.
Had it not been for him San Francisco might never have
been founded in 1776, for it was he who discovered a
way for its first settlers from Sonora overland to California, leading the way with his Indian instinct on a
path that did not as yet exist. That he was a product of
the New World no one can doubt. His father and

grandfather had been Indian fighters like our American Kit Carson. His father had been killed by the Apaches. No one generation could have produced Anza.

The third variety was the most important of all. They were the Franciscans who did more exploration than Anza. There is no doubt as to their ability as explorers, yet it might surprise some to hear them spoken of as a product of the New World. Franciscans, if they come from anywhere, come from Assisi, Italy. Those in New Spain belonged almost too much to Old Spain. The Spanish monarchs had by the Pope been granted special powers over them. The King of Spain paid for their support in the New World, sent them where he wished. In practice at one time he even nominated what individual Franciscans should go where, until a curb was put on that usurped power. Why call them a product of the New World?

Yet the Franciscan explorers of our Southwest did bear a mark of the New World. It was partly that they were identified with a special New World missionary movement that had its fountains of enthusiasm at several Franciscan missionary colleges in Mexico; at Zacatecas, and at Mexico City, and most prominently in the college of Santa Cruz at Querétaro. This last college had been founded by a Father Llinas in 1682 for the special purpose of penetrating into unsettled lands. It sent missionaries south into the wildest parts of South America, and north into North America — into the future United States. It provided a special preparatory training; two hours daily were set aside to the study of Indian languages and of methods of evangelizing those of an Indian culture. Furthermore, as our colleges in the United States now have a rivalry as to which shall win in football, so these colleges, though all Franciscan, and all of the same branch of the Franciscans — the Observantists — competed with one another in establishing what they called their *doctrinas*, that is, missions, in the most difficult and perilous places.

These colleges had a special spirit of their own, and the ardor of that spirit had a special inspiration. That inspiration was to be sure the general Franciscan inspiration, Our Lady, but it was particularly derived from her as Mexico's patroness, Our Lady of Guadalupe, who had in 1531 presented her picture so graciously to the Indian boy. Finally they were also animated by a high regard for the Venerable Maria de Agreda whose words had aroused in many of them their sense of a missionary vocation.

The Venerable Maria de Agreda was a Spanish nun of the early seventeenth century who belonged to the Franciscan order of women which at that time in Spain was known as the Conceptionist Order. She was the Mother Superior of a convent in Agreda, and as superior she was all sagacity, prudence and good sense. She was a practical woman like Saint Theresa of Avila. But also like Saint Theresa of Avila she was an ecstatic. Our Lady, she believed, often spoke to her, telling her of her Immaculate Conception. Our Lady revealed to her also how beautiful it was to be a missionary, how dearly she loved missionaries, how she listened to them and aided them. Maria de Agreda believed that she herself in ecstasy was allowed to be a missionary. She had visited lands in the Far East and had preached to the heathen, and had seen Saint Francis's friars there and could describe them.   Also she had visited another land which on investigation she decided must have been New Mexico, for the friars she saw there and whom she described as having seen there were identified as friars who had been in New Mexico.   She had been a missionary to the Jumanos, the nation whom Cabeza de Vaca had found so strange.

There is no reason why any one should feel that he has to believe that the Venerable Maria de Agreda visited the Jumanos during the 1620's or at any other time, but it is an undisputable fact that the Franciscans of Mexico believed it, that Friar Llinas who founded the missionary college at Querétaro especially believed it, that Friar Junípero Serra, founder of California, believed it, and that the Franciscan explorers who roamed with the "leather-jackets," who were as hardy as they, and even more resourceful, and who went farther than they — even as far as the little salt sea, Sevier Lake in Utah — believed it. They looked on the land they trod as having been trod miraculously by Maria de Agreda.   They received consolation in their hardships and happy unconcern in all danger by remembering what beautiful things concerning their calling had been said by Our Lady of the Immaculate Conception through the same nun.

Of these Franciscan explorers surely he that was most unique was Friar Garcés.   He was unique because he traveled most uniquely — usually alone — solitary from other white companions — associated at one time with an

Indian who had been a fugitive from the missions of
Lower California, but who, like him, loved to be traveling.
He could not bother not to trust either this companion
or any other, or to be frightened at the Indians he encountered when he disappeared into the unknown des-
erts for six months at a time.   He trusted men because
he trusted Our Lady.   A learned man who had been a
professor of theology in the University at Majorca, he
was utterly simple, and in face of any difficulty he merely
unfurled the banner on which Our Lady was pictured
and rode toward it.

In 1775 Friar Garcés started off with Colonel Anza on
his expedition toward San Francisco from Sonora, Mexico, but after the path had been discovered he departed
from the gregariousness of "leather-jackets" and colonists.   Taking two other Indians with him he descended
the Colorado River to its mouth, then ascended it and
began to take a more northerly route back to New Mexico.   He cut across a land which he called "difficult," a
word rare in his vocabulary.   On June 25th, 1776, he
had finished an ascent and went some nine miles through
what he praises as "good ground, with much grass, and
many junipers, pines and other trees."   The next morning he continued south and east, and suddenly came on
the gate of the Grand Cañon of the Colorado.   It is true
that one of Coronado's lieutenants had seen the Cañon
a quarter of a thousand years before, but Friar Garcés
was the first to come at it from the west and to figure out
its significance.   He saw the cliffs.   "And within these,"
he says, "flows the Colorado River. — There is seen a

very great mountain cliff which in the distance looks blue ; and there runs southeast to northwest a pass open to the very base."

Such were the Spanish explorers of our country. With the exception of Vizcaino, who was a merchant and as such looked on with some suspicion, and therefore not permitted for some time to equip his fleet that entered Monterey, all these explorers were soldiers or priests. They belonged to the classes which Spaniards looked on as most Spanish and most worthy. A priest was a priest. A soldier was more than a soldier ; he was a Christian soldier, a crusader, one of a body which had for eight centuries fought in the name of Our Lady of Pillar of Saragossa against the Moors. These soldiers were sometimes men of fierce energy and independence as was De Soto. And in their wilfullness they were sometimes cruel, as De Soto was in at least one massacre. But these men were all of a supernatural making. The world they trod in was more than this world. They never became mere worshippers of their Spanish ruler, or of Spain, or of themselves. There was God above and there was Our Lady. Father Garcés carried her banner ever with him as the only thing he carried. Vizcaino dedicated his expedition along California's coast to Our Lady of Mount Carmel. Cabrillo's pilot prayed to Our Lady of Guadalupe to be delivered from the on-shore wind off Oregon. — "And if God and His Blessed Mother had not miraculously saved them they could not have escaped," he wrote. — De Soto before he left Cuba had made a will. He began the will :

"I order that, wherever I may die, my body shall be

carried to Xeres — to the church of San Miguel and laid in the sepulchre where lies my mother [and then he went on to speak of his other mother].   And in that church I order that of my goods a site and place be bought, where shall be built a chapel, which shall have for its invocation Our Lady of the Conception."

Had these men been simply of this world they might have become able brigands.   Or they might have stayed at home and rotted.   But they would never have been our explorers.   They came to us as men more mysterious than they knew, strong with a light that flashed into noble deed.   They were so alive with the faith that not a part of our land did they touch but that land became forever unsecular.

It was their privilege to name our rivers, mountains, and valleys.   They were not slaves of routine, they felt free to call a river by any appropriate name as they called for a time the Rio Grande the Wild River of the North, but usually, since they lived under heaven, was it not natural to name what was first seen after the saint in heaven who was that day being celebrated ?   Hence, the place-names in our southwest still read like a litany of the saints : San Francisco, Santa Barbara, San Diego, Santa Maria of the Angels of the Portiuncola (now Los Angeles), San Felipe de Albuquerque (now simple Albuquerque), Santa Clara, San Bernadino, San Ildephonso. But all the land really belonged to Our Lady.   That went without saying.   And at times it was said.   There was a man called Mendoza, an army captain, who in December 1683 was making his way from Texas westerly toward the Jumanos on our New Mexican border.

On the seventeenth of the month he was near — so we are told — to the present town of Ballinger, Texas. He called his camp-site Our Lady of the Pillar of Saragossa. Each day he moved on. On the eighteenth his camping-ground became Our Lady of the Immaculate Conception. On the nineteenth it was Our Lady of Solitude, on the twentieth Our Lady of Happy Voyage, on the twenty-first Our Lady of Good Success, on the twenty-second Our Lady of the Rosary, on the twenty-third Our Lady of Good Order, on the twenty-fourth Our Lady of Bethlehem, on the twenty-fifth (the Nativity) Our Lady of the People, on the twenty-sixth Our Lady of Atocha, on the twenty-seventh Our Lady of Guadalupe, on the twenty-eighth Señora de los Remedios — but why go on?

CHAPTER III

LA CONQUISTADORA

THE FIRST permanent Spanish settlement in the United States was established in 1565 by Pedro Menéndez de Avilés at Saint Augustine, Florida. Its founder was a soldier who held at the time an office the most exasperating to its owner of any in all Europe. It was his duty to see that the Spanish Treasure Fleet from the Gulf of Mexico arrived safely at Seville in Spain. This was a responsibility fit more for a demi-god than a mere man. To tell of the importance of the treasure in terms of mere money value is misleading. We have become so used to hearing of the billions of dollars of budgets not balanced and of debts not paid, that millions of anything mean nothing more to us. In the 1560's this treasure of precious metals — silver and gold — was flowing to Spain at the rate of twenty million pounds sterling a year. Let us say, in order to be up to date, *only* twenty million pounds sterling a year. Yet this current, whatever its size may seem to us, had in its day an effect on Europe's financial climate like to that which we are told the Gulf Stream has now on Europe's modern weather climate. It was the very life-blood of the Spanish monarchy. It was Columbus' strange legacy. It was the wherewithal which enabled Spain to play her all-important rôle in the world. Menéndez was in the position of Atlas holding up the sky. To fail would bring all of Spain's starry destiny down — crashing. He had to be sleepless, and sleeplessness always exasperates.

Yet even more exasperating than the anxiety was the nature of the attacks on that Treasure Fleet which he had to ward off. They were formidable, they were dishonest, and they were hypocritical. Hence that exasperation to which a sense of righteous indignation gives added sharpness. The attackers were English ships and French ships sent out by England's Queen Elizabeth, and France's Queen Catherine de Medici, both of which queens needed very badly some of Spain's treasure, and had, for their ambitions, to play the parasite. When they were at war with Spain it was one thing, but usually they were not. And when they were not, they simply encouraged corsairs to do the robbing for them, pardoning them if they were successful and sharing with them the booty. The corsairs whom they encouraged were people with whom they had little sympathy — either England's so-called Protestant Queen or France's so-called Catholic one. They were Protestants, English or French, who were bound into an international organization, and were animated both by a love of booty and a fierce hatred against Catholic Spain. Without any apparent consciousness of insincerity they worked their depredations with a religious zeal. By this they brought an obloquy on the religion they professed. The Spaniards came to regard as a Protestant any one who had no respect for any law human or divine. And if the Spaniards made the name *luteranos* — Lutherans — to be synonymous with pirates — pirates who were hypocrites — they can scarcely be blamed. To have to fight against

such a foe, which was neither fair foe nor even fair
pirate, aroused in Menéndez a fierce decisiveness.

He was an able man and he took measures which
threatened the piracy. He organized a system of con-
voys, saw to it that the Treasure Ships sailed all together
across the ocean at stated intervals. Lest the pirates
waylay them in the Caribbean after they had separated,
he equipped a mosquito fleet in Caribbean waters to
rout out the pirates from their lairs. He succeeded so
well, that the leaders of the pirates, who were men of
high position and great intelligence — I mean those leaders who stayed in Europe at the King's courts, not those
who commanded the ships — decided that a new plan of
attack must be found. They saw that if they could
establish a base for pirates on the Florida coast, by which
runs the Bahama Channel, they could circumvent all of
the carefully laid defense plans of Menéndez. The
Huguenot Coligny arranged, conspirator-like, that a Huguenot fleet under corsair Ribaut should go to occupy
a stronghold in Florida's shore. Queen Catherine of
France pretended not to notice what was going on.
Queen Elizabeth did exactly the same. But both of
them with their backs turned prayed hard to the devil
that not for the corsairs' good, but for their queenly
good, the corsairs might succeed.

The Spanish ambassador in England, De Silva, and the
Spanish ambassador in France, Chantone, knew perfectly
well what was going on. They gave warning, yet
Philip II had so much to do he gave not enough heed.
What heed he did give was forced out of him by
Menéndez. Menéndez knew that the *luteranos* would

have to be forestalled in Florida. It was he who organized an expedition counter to that of the *luteranos*.

Thus, though the King supplied three hundred soldiers
at royal expense, and twenty thousand ducats besides, it
was Menéndez who supplied from private sources one
million ducats. He equipped a flag-ship, the *San Pelayo*,
and nine other vessels besides, containing one thousand
soldiers, and five hundred others, colonists : artisans of
thirty-eight trades, over a hundred agriculturalists,
twenty-seven families of women and children. It was in
June 1565 that he quitted Cádiz — not to be thwarted.

Not to be thwarted ! The winds tried to hold him
back. The storms wrecked half his ships. He arrived
at Puerto Rico. "Wait," he was counselled, "for rein-
forcements." He was not a man to wait. He came to
Florida. Yes, the French Huguenots were there before
him. He warned them to flee. They laughed. He un-
loaded his cannon at St. Augustine, took just time
enough to erect a chapel to Our Lady, Nuestra Señora
de la Leche — it being the day of her nativity. Then he
attacked and annihilated the French. And looked about
him.

That Spanish St. Augustine should have been so
founded with such show of courage, decision, and also
with such drastic shedding of blood — for Menéndez
showed no quarter to the *luteranos* — augured for the
new settlement a future fiery and fierce. Yet St. Augustine, or Florida, had a quite other destiny, and Menéndez
himself can be held accountable for that other destiny.

Menéndez invited the Jesuits to Florida. The General
of the Jesuits was at that time a Spaniard, St. Francis

Borgia, and the order had been founded thirty years back by a Spanish soldier, St. Ignatius, but for the moment they did not stand well with Philip II, and it was not for Spain's earthly glory that he invited them. He asked for them because he really wanted Christian missionaries. When Menéndez wrote letters, as he often did, to Philip II, he used to end them : "May Our Lord guard and make prosper the Catholic Royal Person of your Majesty with increase of great realms and sovereignties, as Christianity has need of, and we, the servants of your Majesty desire." Menéndez was never the speaker of idle words, not even in the ending of a letter. He was direct and literal in his belief that in taking over Florida he was extending Christendom. The natives of Florida were Philip II's subjects. It was for him to see, as an *encomendero* had in theory to see, to their evangelization.

The Jesuits came. He treated them with a gentleman's courtesy, and a Christian layman's forbearance. They were free. They were free to do what they thought best, even if he did not think it best. The Jesuits had a scheme which seemed to him fantastical. They wished to go to the Bay of the Mother of God in Virginia and there conquer the Indians for God without asking him to conquer them for Spain first.

Such a scheme was not without precedent. When Coronado had deserted the Rio Grande Valley in New Mexico, three Franciscans had asked to be allowed to stay on without the soldiery. They felt that they could do more for the Indians without soldiers at their heels to cause quarrels or give bad example. Two of these Franciscans stayed among the pueblos of New Mexico. They were killed. The third of the friars, Friar Padilla, an ex-soldier, preferred to go to Quivira, to Kansas. And there he went, and there he accomplished nothing except what he accomplished by shedding his own blood. There were eye witnesses to his death, other Spaniards and Christian Indians. A troop of Indians, so they said, came towards him as he marched through Kansas, and began to threaten as if with intent to kill. Father Padilla had told his companions to retreat, and then he advanced and knelt down. That was the end.

Seven years later, in 1549, a Dominican had attempted in Florida what Friar Padilla had attempted in Kansas. His name was Father Luis Cancer. He had landed from a boat at Tampa Bay — Charlotte Harbor — and there received a reception that promised well. He was embraced as with affection by an Indian. But then followed swift the catastrophe : he was led up the sandy shore to the rim of verdure and clubbed to death.

The Jesuits knew all about this, and so did Menéndez. But the Jesuits knew that Father Luis Cancer had previously pacified the wildest Indians in Guatemala by entering their region without the complication and inevitable scandal of soldiery. He had been able to accomplish this by sending ahead of him Indians who had been converted already and who sang songs and acted plays representing to the pagan Indians the creation of the world, the Fall of Man, the Incarnation, the Raising of Lazarus. Thus when he had arrived in the hills of Guatemala the Indians knew what a priest was. In Florida on the contrary he had had no introduction, except by the visits of slave-snatchers. Hence in Florida his failure.

The Jesuits would copy his first success. They would be introduced into the region which they called Ajacan on the Bay of the Mother of God — Chesapeake Bay — by the son of a sachem of that region who had been kidnapped by some of Ayllón's men, but who had turned Christian, and seemed to be truly Christian — Luis. They prevailed on Menéndez to let them try their chances. He lent them a ship.

On September 11, 1570, the ship arrived at Chesapeake Bay. It sailed up the Potomac River, veered into the little Aquia Creek, and then turned home.

The Jesuits were now alone, alone with Luis on a strange shore, on which lived the Indians to whom Luis was to introduce them. There was a party of nine to be introduced. There was Father de Segura, the Jesuit superior who had conceived the expedition, there was Father de Quiros, and there were three lay-brothers and three catechists, and there was one errand boy, Alonzo — Alonzito — son of one of Florida's colonists. They started through mud and swamps toward the Rappahannock River, southward from the Potomac, carrying their supplies. Soon Luis introduced them to some of his countrymen, but it was a bit sinister that not one of the friends of their friend Luis lent a hand with the luggage : they simply stalked along with Indian reserve.

When they came to what was really Luis's country — a day's journey on — they found that it had suffered six years of famine. The Jesuits carried on their shoulders two barrels of biscuits — reserve for the winter. The

Indians, friends of Luis, ate the reserve. The Jesuits built a chapel — the chapel of Our Lady of Ajacan. The Indian friends of Luis seemed but little concerned with the chapel.

Luis disappeared. Before he disappeared his morals had changed and one reason he disappeared was to hide that change. — Luis had shame. — He went to live at a distance from the Fathers whose presence reminded him of that shame. As winter came on Father Quiros and two catechists went after Luis, not with hope to reform his morals but with hope to buy some maize. There still remained some last-summer maize among these Indians and the Jesuits had some trinkets of brass wherewith to pay for it.

Father Quiros and the two catechists never returned from the trip toward Luis. All that returned from the three was their clothing! Luis, the apostate, put on Father Quiros's robe. He was wearing this robe as a uniform when he advanced toward the chapel where the other Jesuits were waiting for the Indian corn. After him came a file of his companions. In a few minutes another five Jesuits had been killed.

Only one was left alive, little Alonzo. After the death of his companions he had the courage to beg of Luis that he might bury his friends. Luis was still Christian enough to give permission. And some of the Indians helped. "They then dug a great trench and buried them side by side, each with his crucifix in his hand, Father Segura first and then all the others in order." And there they sleep and were not even awakened when three hundred years later the Battle of Bull

Run was fought over them, and there they still sleep, still undiscovered — the Spanish cemetery by the Rappahannock.

It was in February that they died. Spring came, and when the first spring leaf-buds were making a green and red haze on the banks of the Potomac, a ship from Menéndez arrived to find the Jesuits. It did not find them.

Governor Menéndez did not wash his hands of the affair with an exclamation : "I told you so." The corsairs were about Cuba like sharks. The French *luteranos* had attacked Havana. And the English *luteranos* had attacked St. Augustine. He had no ships to spare. But he sent back one of them to rescue Alonzito who was reported to be alive. And he found Alonzo.

It seemed as if the generosity of Menéndez to the missionaries was now making him into a missionary. Four years later he was in Spain gathering a fleet together for service in the English Channel. He looked wistfully toward Florida and wrote a letter to his nephew Menéndez Marquez who had succeeded him as Florida's governor. "After the salvation of my soul, there is nothing I desire more than to be in Florida and there end my days saving souls."

Menéndez never returned to Florida. He died the next year, still in Spain, still at work organizing an Armada to beat back the *luteranos*. The Jesuits whom he had invited to Florida, quitted it, going to Mexico. Yet Spain itself took over the vocation which he had desired for himself : that of saving souls in Florida — Indian souls.

In the Florida which Spain occupied, which included our present Florida and the seacoast of Georgia and of

South Carolina under the name of Orista, and also a section of western Georgia under the name of Apalache, there were at the most one hundred thousand natives. All these the King of Spain treated as his subjects, and they looked on him as their sovereign. There were no Spaniards acting as *encomenderos* in Florida to stand between the Indians and their King. The caciques of the various tribes were the *encomenderos* entrusted by the King of Spain with ruling for him their subjects. Some of these caciques actually corresponded by letter with the King, so Hispanicized did they become, but for the most part they remained illiterate and distant. Whenever there was a new governor appointed at St. Augustine twenty-seven caciques used regularly to arrive to make obeisance to him. Their relations with St. Augustine were often very cordial, and more than once they came to St. Augustine's help when St. Augustine was starving. St. Augustine was a fort which, though small, did hold off the English and the French for two hundred years. It also remained a tiny settlement of two hundred Spanish colonists. But most of all it was the capital, political and spiritual, of an Indian commonwealth.

The King not only protected these Indians and tried to keep peace among them, he sent to them Franciscans, whom he paid for, himself, at the rate of 115 ducats a year. There were usually between twenty and thirty Franciscans in Spanish Florida, who established in all some fifty *doctrinas* or missions, though all did not exist at any one time. From these *doctrinas* or permanent missions, the Franciscans had other stations which they

visited at intervals. Their results were not startling.
They could not be. At no one time were there more
than twelve thousand baptized Indians in Florida. Yet
the influence of the Franciscans was very great. It
layed the beginning of an Indian civilization agricultural
and religious in nature, which lasted on until the aggressive and commercial civilization of the Carolina English
harried and demolished it.

Long before the English took Florida in 1763 this
civilization had succumbed. And by the time we, the
United States, succeeded to England in Florida it had
disappeared as completely as a lost Atlantis. Yet even
now records of it here and there come to light that astonish us. We discover, for instance, that a Father
Pareja wrote a half-dozen books in the Timucuan Florida
tongue in 1612, and had them printed in Mexico —
among them *La Doctrina Christiana*, *Catechismo*, and
Confesionario — and that he and his colleagues were
sometimes in two months able to teach the Indians to
read. Florida Indians were writing letters one to another eight years before the Indians of Massachusetts
stared at the first English Pilgrims at Plymouth.

The same Father Pareja made in the same year, 1612,
a report to the Council of the Indies concerning the
quality of his Indian converts :

"Very many persons are found, men and women, who
confess their sins and who receive Holy Communion
with tears and who compare advantageously with many
Spaniards. And I shall make bold to say and sustain my
contention by what I have learned from experience that

with regard to the mysteries of faith many of them answer better than the Spaniards because the latter are careless in these matters."

But lest it be thought that good Father Pareja was gullible, let us call in other testimony. In 1696 an English Quaker, Jonothan Dickenson, made an unwilling visit to Florida, and there saw and bore witness to the good that the Spaniards were accomplishing. The cause of his visit was shipwreck. His ship, called curiously enough the *Reformation*, had been cast up useless on the Florida shore fifty miles south of St. Augustine. With him were his wife, children, five negro slaves and one little negro slave girl called Venus. He and his family were not massacred by the Indians who met him on the shore. Was he an Englishman, a Nichaleer as they called Englishmen, that is a corsair? Dickenson told a pardonable lie and said he was Spanish. He was brought to the Spaniards at St. Augustine and there at the anti-English fort was treated with a courtesy and charity he could not foresee.

He came to a mission called "Santa Cruce." There he found the usual Indian warehouse, built round, having within it sixteen squares, in each of which squares there was a small cabin built for two persons — the house being about fifty feet in diameter. In its middle was an opening in the roof "about fifteen feet," the house was "very clean," and a fire was made near his cabin.

"In this town," goes on Dickenson, "they have a friar, and a large house to worship in with three bells; and the Indians go as constantly to their devotions at all times and seasons as any of the Spaniards. Night being come and the time of devotions over, the Friar came in, and many of the Indians both men and women, and they had a dance according to their way and custom."

Then Quaker Dickenson goes on, and I continue to quote him, for his book is not found in every library :

"At St. Wan's (San Juan) they have a friar and a worship-house. The people are very industrious, having plenty of hogs and tooles, and large crops of corn, as we could tell by their corn-houses."

Then he described the largest of the missions : "At St. Mary's the ware-house was 81 feet in diameter, built round, with 32 squares, in each square a painted cabin, eight feet long. The women that were of these towns cloath themselves with the moss of trees, making gowns and petticoats thereof, which at the distance or in the night looks very neat. The Indian boys are kept to school in the Church, the friar being their schoolmaster. This town was the largest of all, and about a mile from it was St. Philip."

So Dickenson proceeded on from Spanish Florida to English Charleston and there — it should be recorded — his Spanish escort was received with a gratitude they deserved. They were feasted for eight days and "paid 100 pieces of 8."

There is another bit of evidence as to what the Spaniards were doing in Florida. In the middle of the seventeenth century the Franciscans at the request of the Apalache Indians established missions among that tribe in northwest Florida. There were thirty thousand of these Indians and seven *doctrinas* were founded among them. Because they were so far inland and so little was said of them, it might be imagined by us that the work among them was futile or perfunctory. But after half a century the English and their Indian allies from South Carolina attacked these missions, burned a friar at the stake, and led off a thousand Indians into slavery. The remaining Indians fled to the French settlements in Louisiana, to Biloxi, Mississippi, and the French gave a description of them after they arrived there.

Pénicaut, an ensign of the French navy, was the describer:

"The Apalaches have public services like the Catholics of France. Their great feast is Saint Louis's day. On the eve they come to invite the officers of the fort to festivities in their village, and they offer good cheer that day to all who come, especially the French.

"The priests of our fort go there to say the High Mass, which they hear with much devotion, chanting the psalms in Latin as they do in France, and after dinner Vespers and Benediction of the Blessed Sacrament. The men wear a kind of cloth coat, and the women mantles, petticoats of silk in French style, except that they wear no head-dresses, going bare-headed. Their long, jet-black hair is plaited and hangs down the back in one or two plaits such as Spanish girls wear. Those whose hair is too long, turn it up to the middle of the back and tie it with ribbon.

"They have a church where one of our French priests goes on Sundays and holidays to say Mass. They have a baptismal font to baptize their children, and a cemetery beside their church, with a cross erected, and there they bury their dead."

Spain in Florida, because of her exasperation, had every reason to think only of Spain, and of exerting violence in Spain's cause, yet she ended up doing what she did almost entirely for the Indians. And the same happened elsewhere.

Thirty-three years after the settling of Florida New Mexico was settled. Its founder, the man that corresponded to Florida's Menéndez, was Oñate. He was a rich mine owner of Zacatecas in Mexico — seat of the famous silver mines and of a Franciscan missionary college. — He had married a wife who was descended from both Cortez and Montezuma, and in entering New Mexico he was wishing to be both a conqueror and an emperor. He even asked of the King of Spain that he might be a viceroy of New Mexico, independent of New Spain's viceroy. This was refused him, but he was allowed to be governor of it, and to hand on the governorship of it to his heirs. So he started off from Zacatecas in 1598 with four hundred Spaniards (one hundred and thirty of them with families), and ten Franciscan friars besides, and eighty-three two-wheeled carts, their wheels made of solid disks of wood, and seven thousand cattle. He was looking for power, of course, and adventure, perhaps, and certainly honor, but he would never have started if he had not heard from previous explorers that there was silver to the north. He was different from Menéndez in that he set much store on *bonanza* — prosperity. He was another individualist with thoughts originally not too spiritual.

Oñate never found his *bonanza*. He established the one considerable Spanish colony within the limits of the

United States. Santa Fé became its capital with its four thousand inhabitants, its beautifully ceilinged three churches, its spacious fiesta-loving plaza, its long, low, arcaded governor's palace. It was not a colony to scoff at. It was not rich, for though there are mines in New Mexico's earth, the Spaniards never developed them. They lived by sheep, cattle, agriculture, and song and dance. But it was a unique colony : for three hundred and fifty years it lasted in utter isolation till the Yankee traders arrived from Missouri with New England wares which they could sell for ten times their New England price. It was Christendom's farthest colony, so far from its home-land, Spain, that the voyage to it took a year. Even to go to Mexico City took five months, and was attended with grave peril from Indians. It was so separate from the rest of the world that it developed its own religious art, painted its own pictures, carved its own statues, developed its own dances.

But the most extraordinary thing about New Mexico is not its comparative success as a Spanish colony, but its success as a Spanish realm which contained two cultures, Indian and Spanish, both of them Christian. There were in the Rio Grande Valley in New Mexico when the Spaniards arrived some two score so-called pueblos. These pueblos were each a cluster of mud-built houses, set shoulder to shoulder and piled one upon the other up to five stories. These structures were fortresses to their occupants against the Apaches and Navahoes and Comanches, who as the old chronicler Benăvides said, surrounded them on all sides "for an illimitable distance." But also these cities were strongholds of a proud tradi-

tion, temples of an elaborate religious cult, with a liturgical calendar dearly guarded ; they represented a culture
which the Spaniards might well have mocked at, like
many a Yankee of the last century, and might have destroyed in an attempt to make its owners Spaniards. Instead they Christianized it, and left it Indian.

Of course, it was the Spanish Franciscans who mainly
accomplished this, but without some cooperation from
the colonists their efforts would have been frustrated.
The Franciscans taught the Indians to know the story of
Creation by having them act it themselves, and the story
of man's more marvellous remaking by having them
dance their Indian dances before the crib of Our Saviour.
As for the Spaniards they no more mocked at the Indians
than the Indians mocked at them. And we have the
sight of two cultures existing side by side, both Christian,
both saluting each other with Christian salutations, both
celebrating Our Lady of Guadalupe in their own way,
yet except for that bond utterly different.

The next part of the United States to be occupied by
Spain after New Mexico was Texas. The entry there
did not come till one hundred years after Oñate's entry
into New Mexico. The motive behind the entry was
even more unromantically mundane than had been that
of Menéndez or that of Oñate. It was simply to keep
another Catholic country, France, from coming too near
to the silver mines of New Spain. The leader of the
expedition was Alonso de León, governor of Coahuila,
who had but one aim, to find out where the French were,
fight them if necessary, burn their fort, and then see that
they did not return.

But with León went, as usual, a Franciscan, Friar Massenet, who was as more than usually up in the clouds as León was more than usually down to the ground. Friar Massenet had been educated at the College of the Holy Cross at Querétaro, especially for the missions, and there he had heard of the visions of the Venerable Maria de Agreda. He believed that she had really made her "flights" to Texas, he believed that the Texas Indians were waiting for him. As he rode into Texas with León across the Rio Grande up toward Louisiana he kept scrutinizing the Indians to discern some sign that they had received supernatural visits from that extraordinary nun, and in his enthusiasm he was sure that he detected many signs of it.

It was the spirit of Friar Massenet rather than that of Alonso de León that became predominant in Texas. For a hundred years the youthfulness of the Franciscans continued — it never waned. On the other hand the motive that brought the soldiers soon disappeared. The French abandoned Texas, and the Spanish soldiers became a mere escort to the Spanish friars. They became a police force, and a very shadowy one, there being in it for all of Texas but one hundred men. Texas became a Franciscan province important only for its *doctrinas* or missions, of which there were sometimes seven in existence, sometimes ten, of which there were, in all, founded twenty-five. Spain did have its political capital there, as it had in Florida and in New Mexico. At first the capital was a mere fort near Louisiana, in the northeast corner of our State, Nuestra Señora del Pilar de los Adaeds. Afterwards it became a settled little city on the San Antonio River, San Fernando, to which colonists had been laboriously brought from the Canary Islands. But the missions were more important than the cities. San Fernando has ceased to be called San Fernando, which is forgotten. It is now San Antonio, Texas, named after the mission that was once beside that city, and is still remembered.

The mission buildings of Florida had been made of a kind of oyster-shell cement known as tabby : they had not been impressive to the eye. The missions of New Mexico had been built of the reddish tawny adobe like the pueblos. They had been beautiful. The missions of Texas were equally beautiful and, being nearer Europe, more elaborate. Also, simply as ranches they had their importance. In 1750 the missions had passed their heydey but San Antonio even then possessed "115 gentle horses, 200 mares with their stallions, 15 donkeys, 18 mules, 1115 head of cattle, 50 yoke of oxen, 2200 head of sheep and goats." And there were crops too — corn, beans, red pepper and cotton. But the converts of all these beautiful missions were never very numerous ; they numbered at no time more than one or two thousand. At San Antonio where the inventory cited above was made, the Christian Indians at the mission were but 186 — seventy-five others being still unbaptized. The beauty of the Texas ruins witness not so much to the beauty of a Franciscan success, as to the beauty of the perpetual Franciscan hopefulness.

The spirit of Father Massenet survived disaster after disaster. The disasters were not easily avoidable. Texas was filled with many warring tribes, of many warring cultures. To establish a mission for one tribe meant to draw the enmity of another. Thus the work was endless. It had to be begun and begun, over and over again. Yet it kept on being begun. As late as 1793 the Franciscans were building a new mission. No longer could they rely on the King for funds, but a rich lady, the Countess of Valenciana, supplied them. No longer could they rely on their own dear Spain, even, for future favor. Their missions were being secularized. That is, they and the Indians were being robbed on the advice of well-meaning philosophers for the benefit of ill-meaning profiteers. Yet they did not heed the storm-signal. Once again in that late year when the whole world seemed to be becoming irreligious they established a new outpost, at the confluence of the San Antonio and Guadalupe Rivers, and named it as they named most of their missions after Our Lady, Nuestra Señora del Refugio.

The fourth of the regions of our land occupied by the Spanish was Arizona. It too became an Indian commonwealth for the reason that it was never anything else. No mundane motive at all entered into its founding. It did not have to be transformed from a material to a spiritual enterprise. Father Kino, the Tyrolean-born Jesuit, was its founder. He made the entry, made the pacifications, built the missions, not exactly with his own money, but with money received entirely from private sources. The royal paternalism merely gave him permission to go beyond the Spanish Mexican settlements and conquer the Indians with charity for arms. On April 21st, 1700, he started forth from the Mission of Our Lady of Sorrows in Sonora on his way to found his first mission in

Arizona. He had ten Indians with him, and fifty-three horses and mules. Four days later he arrived near our Tucson, in a country which in those days was called New Biscay — Nueva Biscaya. "On the twenty-eighth," writes Father Kino, "we began the foundations of a very large and spacious church and house of San Xavier del Bac, all the many people working with much pleasure and zeal, some in excavating for the foundations, others in hauling many and very good stones of tezontle from a little hill which was about a quarter of a league away. For the mortar for these foundations it was not necessary to carry water, because by means of irrigation ditches we very easily conducted the water where we wished. And that house, with its court and garden nearby, will be able to have throughout the year all the water it may need, running to any place or workroom one may please." This was Jesuitry.

It was also a plan of Jesuitry to occupy our California (called in the old days Upper California to distinguish it from the peninsula still Mexico's which was Lower California), but the plan had no consummation, for the Jesuits were suppressed in the Spanish dominions in 1763 by the able Bourbon king, Charles III, who wanted to be even more able.

It was this same King who must be thanked for occupying this California which the Jesuits whom he suppressed wanted to occupy. His motive was not to fulfill what the Jesuits wanted to do. It was less spiritual. He was afraid that the Russians would occupy California. They had indeed already begun to do so. So, not having many soldiers, he gave the work of occupation to the

Franciscans. And they in utter spiritual unconcern took the work, forgot the Russians, who in the meantime had disappeared, and made the work theirs.

The expedition that conducted the Franciscans to California belonged to the King. It had soldiers with it, and supplies, and colonists — all provided at the King's command by the Viceroy Bucarelli. But it was not the King who is celebrated as the founder of Spanish California. It is Father Junípero Serra, who took the King's expedition and spiritualized it. He was not disobedient, or arrogant. He merely obeyed the King's perfectly pious phrases and was not particularly interested in other more political motives in the King's mind : they were not his affairs. Yet he with his ardor animated the voyage of occupation, and with his completely supernatural motive gave a consequence to it that the King would never have dreamed.

We all know how the occupation would have been abandoned except for him. Not all the military and naval plans went wholly well. In 1769 when Friar Junípero had established himself at San Diego and when he had been there six months Portolá, the "leather-jacket" military commander, ordered a retreat. Scurvy and famine and Indian hostility made retreat advisable. "Give me nine days," begged Father Junípero. On the ninth day it would be St. Joseph's Day, the 19th of March. If by then relief ships had not arrived let the order to retreat be obeyed.

The ninth day arrived. No ships. "Carry me to the hill." Father Junípero was too weak to walk, but not too weak to pray. By sunset a ship was seen and the colony and mission were not abandoned.

California did not become an important military post. It did not have to. Nor did it become simply twenty-one missions, containing thirty thousand Christian Indians, extending as a "procession" — to use the expression of Friar Junípero — for six hundred miles. It became a mirage, incredible yet true, substantial yet impossible.

In 1827 an Italian circumnavigator of the globe caught sight of Santa Barbara. "As we advanced the buildings of the mission appeared under a finer aspect. From the roadstead we could have taken it for a castle of mediæval times, with its lofty windows, belfry, and watch-tower. Coming nearer, the building appears larger, and without losing any of its beauty, takes on, little by little, a religious aspect ; the turret becomes a spire : the cross, instead of announcing a knight's arrival, sounds the office of the Angelus : the first illusion disappears, and behold the castle is a convent."

The Yankees who sailed from Boston around Cape Horn saw this mirage also and also were fascinated by it, and were impressed not only by its beauty but by its prosperity. They investigated it as if to find whether or not it were a mere mirage and when they found that it was not and that they could trade with it, which meant that it was absolutely real, they were doubly fascinated. In 1829 Alfred Robinson of Boston visited the mission of San Luis Rey, and wrote an account of it in sober admiration, through which shone vaguely a respect even for the religious life of the friars.

"This Mission," wrote Robinson, "was founded in the year 1798, by its present minister, Father Antonio Peyri, who has been for many years a reformer and director among the Indians. At this time (1829) its population was about three thousand Indians, who were all employed in various occupations. Some were engaged in agriculture, while others attended to the management of over sixty thousand head of cattle. Many were carpenters, masons, coopers, saddlers, shoemakers, weavers, etc., while the females were employed in spinning and preparing wool for their looms, which produced a sufficiency of blankets for their yearly consumption. Thus every one had his particular vocation, and each department its official superintendent, or alcalde ; these were subject to the supervision of one or more Spanish Mayordomos, who were appointed by the missionary father, and consequently under his immediate direction.

"The building occupies a large square, of at least eighty or ninety yards each side ; forming an extensive area, in the centre of which a fountain constantly supplies the establishment with pure water. The front is protected by a long corridor, supported by thirty-two arches, ornamented with latticed railings, which, together with the fine appearance of the church on the right, presents an attractive view to the traveller ; the interior is divided into apartments for the missionary and mayordomos, store-rooms, workshops, hospitals, rooms for the unmarried males and females, while near at hand is a range of buildings tenanted by families of the superintendents. There is also a guard house, where were stationed some ten or a dozen soldiers, and in the rear spacious granaries stored with an abundance of wheat, corn, beans, peas, etc., also large enclosures for wagons, carts, and the implements of agriculture. In the interior of the square might be seen the various trades at work, presenting a scene not dissimilar to some of the working departments of our state prisons. Adjoining are two large gardens which supply the table with fruit and vegetables and two or three large 'ranches' or farms are situated from five to eight leagues distant, where the Indians are employed in cultivation and domesticating cattle.

"The Church is a large, stone edifice whose exterior is not without some considerable ornament and tasteful finish ; but the interior is richer and the walls are adorned with a variety of pictures of saints and Scripture. Subjects glaringly coloured and attractive to the eye. Around the altar are many images of the saints, and the tall and massive candelabras, lighted during Mass, throw an impressive light on the whole."

It is strange whatever enterprise the Spaniards attempted within our borders turned to gold — not earthly but spiritual gold. — It would seem as if beyond the southern boundaries of our country northward the more earthly motives could not go. This phenomenon can be partly explained by the homeliest of reasons, such as that the regions had very little earthly appeal to the Spaniards. But also we must in fairness thank the Spanish monarchs, for they were responsible for all Spanish doings in all America.

In Spain the Spanish kings were very little absolute. They had Spanish individualism to battle against, and Spanish philosophy with its strong and outspoken bias against tyranny to keep them in check. Also they had the independence of the Church to respect ; and they had the various corporative rights of various groups of their subjects to be wary of. In the New World it was different. All — at least on paper — was in their hands. They could nominate bishops, collect tithes, send missionaries this way or that. All affairs of government were, of course, in their hands, as also were all affairs of trade. They played the omnipotent fathers of the New World, trying to rule and advise their children in all things, thereby involving themselves in an endless correspondence in which in spite of all help from others and all their own industry, they fell hopelessly behind.

It is not a question here in this book of whether it was right or wrong to repose such responsibility in one man. It is certain that the Pope has never given such a spiritual responsibility to any lay-rulers as he gave after the discovery of America to the Spanish kings, and it is obviously not a papal custom so to do. It was a makeshift in the extraordinary emergency of a New World rising out of the ocean when the Papacy was crippled. But leaving all that aside, the Spanish kings did much better than human beings can usually be relied on to do. In our land they poured in much treasure for a purpose which, nationalistically or in terms of their dynasty, was useless. They never forgot that if the Pope had given them strange powers he had honored them with strange responsibilities. They became, without hypocrisy or affectation or simulation, the patrons and supporters of missionaries. Symbolically, Queen Isabella had given her first gold from America to gild the ceiling of the west apse of Santa Maria Maggiore at Rome.

To support a Franciscan friar costs as much as to support a soldier, yet the Spanish monarchs during the seventeenth century maintained over three thousand friars constantly in the New World. And they were but one of the many orders of religions who worked there at royal behest.

But in 1760 the Spanish monarch performed an act which is significant : he handed over his Spain and all its possessions (including of course half our land) to Our Lady, to her Immaculate Conception. In so doing he merely indicated that she had already been long in charge. She had always found more obedience in the King's subjects than he himself. She had owned their better natures. She had been more imperious. She had gently taken command. She had had her way. It was in her name, and in response to her that the real conquest by the Spaniards of our lands took place. In 1680 there had been a revolt in New Mexico by the Pueblo Indians. Not for thirteen years could the Spaniards return to Santa Fé. When under De Vargas they did return, it was as Christians they moved, Christian Indians, Christian Spaniards, against other Indians who momentarily had turned apostate. And De Vargas, as if realizing the truth of this, carried with him as his leader Our Lady — that is, a statue of Our Lady, Our Lady of Victory, La Conquistadora. He set this statue in a little wagon as he marched up from El Paso, up the Rio Grande northward, and as he moved it must have pitched and rocked as it dived into and came out of the ravines and arroyos. As he drew near to Santa Fé, the old capital, he made a vow to Our Lady, La Conquistadora, that if she gave him victory, he would every year have her statue carried about Santa Fé's Plaza in a procession. The victory was won, bloodlessly, and the statue three hundred and fifty years later continues every year to be carried about that plaza. The conquest of a third of the United States by the Spaniards had never been punitive. It had largely been spiritual. There had been no supreme, lordlylike conquistador. Its most important conquistador had been La Conquistadora.

CHAPTER IV

FATHER MARQUETTE

IN THE year 1638, Oxenstiern, the Swedish Ambassador at the court of Louis XIII of France, wrote a letter to the celebrated Hollander, Grotius, the jurist, telling him of an event which had recently taken place and which could excite only his derision.

"The King," he says, speaking of Louis XIII, "has consecrated both his person and his kingdom to the Blessed Virgin, from the beginning of this year on. He has no doubt but that the prosperous issue of his last campaign is a result of this consecration : Not content with erecting an altar in the Cathedral of this city (Paris) which will cost four hundred thousand 'livres,' he has decided to have celebrated with more solemnity than heretofore the feast which they call the Assumption of the Virgin. To this purpose he has sent forth letters patent to Parliament."

Oxenstiern was right. Louis XIII had done exactly what the Ambassador said. He had done it seriously, publicly, and not as a pious gesture. Oxenstiern and Grotius — Protestants both — laughed. The eighteenth century of skepticism would look back at the act and mock. Le Vassor, the historian, in whose works published in 1708 I happened to read the letter, was more than mocking : he was indignant. The nineteenth century on the other hand would find it difficult even to be impatient at it, it was of so little account. Yet by the great body of Frenchmen in 1638 it was taken seriously indeed. Had it not been treated as an important affair, Oxenstiern would never have thought it worth writing about. France was very especially and very officially consecrated to Our Lady in the year 1638.

It happened to be that at this time France was beginning to play the prominent rôle in the world which had hitherto been played by Spain. It was but five years after this that her armies at Rocroi defeated at last the moving battlements of the Spanish infantry which had been an ambulatory and invincible fortress in Europe for a hundred and fifty years. France, which had been re-disciplined into unity by Cardinal Richelieu, was about to assume the military hegemony in the Old World which had long been Spain's. Also in the New World she was beginning to compete with Spain. The Spanish dreams, like a flock of birds scared by a hunter, had gone migratory and settled in France.

It was significant that she began her new destiny by entrusting it to the Blessed Virgin, the same Our Lady of Victories whom De Vargas had hailed to be the "Conquistadora" of New Mexico. As Spain came to the New World with a sense of a Divine Mandate, so France came to the New World with the sense that she was assuming or reassuming a Christian vocation, for France's consecration to Our Lady was not merely an appeal for help : it was an offer of service.

France's gate of entry into the New World was the St. Lawrence River with Quebec at its mouth, on the banks of which grew up Canada. From our point of view, Canada has an analogy with Mexico. If we face south, we see a Mexico from which the Spaniards explored for us half our country. Mexico was the Spanish door to our interior. If we look north we see Canada from which the French explored the other half of it. Canada was our country's other side door: the French one.

The French explorers entering by their northern door almost evenly matched what the Spaniards performed from the South. Their methods, however, had to be entirely different, for their equipment was not the same, and their wealth was less, and their royal patronage less important, and, above all, they came upon utterly different geographic conditions. The Spaniards arrived in our country with horses, and the roads they looked for were roads which horses could use. In the Florida swamps such roads did not exist. Even in the Carolinas and Alabama where the ground was firm to horses' hoofs, the forests made horse-travel difficult. Yet horse-travel remained the Spanish means of travel, and in the Great Plains across the Mississippi, and in New Mexico on the dry tufic soil amid the scattered low junipers, the ideal road for horses was found. Thus to the Spanish explorer dry open land was what was asked for. Rivers might be convenient as a horse-trough, and the Mississippi served as a road of escape for De Soto's men when their horses could serve them no more, but, for the most part, rivers were a hindrance. Their channels in the West were so many abysses that barred the way. Their swamps and currents in the southeast were so many moats tediously to be forded, often to be swum.

But the rivers were the French roads. The French explorers took their hint from the wonderful river-road of the St. Lawrence stretching so straight three hundred miles southwest from Quebec. The St. Lawrence started them as river-farers, and they never ceased so to be. They had no horses; their steeds were the Algonquian birch-bark canoes, which were but twelve feet long, and so light they could be carried when a waterfall too great to leap stood ahead of them. As thunder-storms are said to follow watercourses, so they followed our creeks and our rivers, and the flooding widespread of the rivers where they became lakes. They balanced and bucked on the rapids. They plodded with weary paddles against the chop of the inland seas. Up streams they labored and when the water became too shallow, they waded and dragged their canoes after them. And when the head-waters became still shallower, when the river turned into a source, a marsh, then they carried their canoes, and carried what they had carried in the canoes, to the next riverhead, or the next lake. Wherever the rivers led there was no stopping the French.

And where did the rivers from Quebec not lead ?   The French knew no Alleghanies to bar them from the West. The long majestic-wide St. Lawrence cut its valley north of those mountains. It linked the Atlantic Ocean with the Great Lakes, even with extremest Lake Superior, which extended its shining oak-leaf of water to halfway across our continent. And from the Great Lakes south it was but a short canoe-carry to the south-ward-flowing rivers which led to the Gulf of Mexico.

The rivers served the French as the great plains served the Spanish and served them even better.

It is possible to praise the exploring of the French by counting the States that they were the first to enter, from Montana to Maine. Maine is theirs, New Hampshire theirs, and Vermont, New York, New Jersey, Pennsylvania, Ohio, Indiana, Michigan, Illinois, Iowa, Missouri, Wisconsin, Minnesota, the Dakotas, Montana. Other States, first explored by the Spaniards, they re-explored : Tennessee, Alabama, Mississippi, Louisiana, Arkansas, Nebraska. But a list of States tells no story. The greatness of French exploration cannot be expressed in a list of States. The French explorers have their glory because they discovered the great secret of our country, the Mississippi system. They discovered what makes us an organism. It was a discovery similar to that of discovering that a man had a spinal column. There is a suspense in us as we look back and see them fumbling for it. We hold our breath as if we are watching a child's game.

The first who fumbled for it was Champlain. Champlain was of that portion of the French nation who took seriously the consecration of France to the Blessed Virgin. Brought up as a Huguenot, he had returned to the fullness of the faith with an enthusiasm no less ardent because it was coupled with a rare discretion and a forbearance towards those who did not share his enthusiasm. It was he who invited the Franciscans of the Recollect branch to New France as missionaries. It was he who on his deathbed left a large part of his wealth to the Jesuits (who never received it). It was he who as Governor of Quebec conducted his fort under Quebec's rock as a semi-monastic community. It was in 1608 that he had founded Quebec, and it was before Louis XIII had made Oxenstiern grimace by dedicating France to Notre Dame that he died. Yet he was of that France which took its religious vocation as its most important vocation.

Champlain never discovered the Mississippi. He would have been a most appropriate explorer of it, for he was above all a geographer. As a governor he was above the average because of his integrity. As a trader, perhaps even because of his integrity, he was of little use. As a geographer he was supreme. He was never quite at peace with himself except when finding a new way somewhere, and making a map of it.

He began his pathfinding in the Atlantic Ocean, investigating places already known though improperly mapped. At one time more than any one in the world he was acquainted with our New England shore. He mapped Plymouth Harbor and called it St. Louis almost a generation before the English Pilgrims settled it. He was an excellent navigator, and safely investigated the tide rips and shoals on the outer elbow of Cape Cod. But the St. Lawrence River and French patriotism turned him into a riverman. It was not that he was really interested in rivers. He followed the rivers in order to find the sea — Balboa's south ocean — the Spanish Sea. Concerning this it seemed to him that the Indians of New France were trying to give information when they talked about the great water to the west. It is scarcely conceivable that they really were, for though the Indians were great wanderers, thinking nothing of a thousand-mile journey,

and were great passers-on of information and of legends,
there was between them and the Pacific the Rocky
Mountains as a road-end and a screen. Almost surely
what they were fabling about was the Great River, the
Mississippi. Without knowing it Champlain was a
searcher for our vertebral column, the Mississippi.

He did not find the Great River, though he might have,
if he had not made enemies of the Iroquois Indians who
controlled the Upper St. Lawrence and who possessed
Lake Ontario as their lake. Because he had fired on them
on Lake Champlain, touching three of them with one shot
of his arquebus and killing, of those three, one, and because he had made friends with their enemies, the Algonquins and the Hurons, they barred the direct road to the
Mississippi to him and to the French. He tried to break
the blockade; with a party of Hurons he even attacked the
Iroquois capital in New York State on Lake Onondaga,
but to no effect. He merely succeeded in sharpening the
Iroquois hostility. So he never took the canoe-path of
the St. Lawrence to Ontario, never, as it was obvious to
do, came to the Niagara River and listened to the thunder
of Erie's waters pouring into Ontario. He never came to
Erie at all, from whence he would have been able to cross
northward to the headwaters of the Ohio, and float a
thousand miles or so downstream into the Mississippi.
Because of the Iroquois his excursions were deflected
to the north of the St. Lawrence, up the Saguenay to
nowhere, or up the Ottawa to the northeast corner of
Lake Huron, Georgian Bay. The latter route could lead
toward the Mississippi, but it was a detour and too long a
detour for Champlain in his remaining years to take.

The next Frenchman who might have found the Mississippi was Etienne Brulé. He had not the virtue to deserve much good luck. But he was one of those picturesque characters who often arrive both in storybooks and in real life where their betters do not. Brulé was a man of infinite resource, and of unprincipled stratagems, of unexpected and sometimes disobedient digressions; he might well have blundered on the Mississippi while being sent in the opposite direction.

He did have a sender — the sender being Champlain. He was known even as one of Champlain's "young men." These young men were not his offspring, but he had provided them with a special nurture so that they could continue the exploration that he dreamed of. This nurture consisted of living with the Indians as an Indian when one was young enough to be able to learn their ways and their language, and be, as far as woodcraft and hardihood went, a savage. This training had made of Brulé a man clever enough to trick both Indians and White Men.

In 1616 when Champlain was planning to punish the Iroquois and take their palisaded village on Lake Onondaga, he gave orders to clever Brulé to go round the west end of Lake Ontario, round the west flank of the Iroquois and arrive at the enemies of the Iroquois to the southwest. Let him bring up some of these enemies as his allies to the rear of the Iroquois.

No one will really ever know what Brulé saw and did. He was not a complete pagan: he wore an *Agnes Dei* round his neck, and on one occasion — to save his own life — preached a sermon on God's power to the Indians. Neither was he a renegade Frenchman, though later he let himself be forced by the English corsair Kerk, into piloting the English ships up the St. Lawrence to capture Quebec. But he told and did what was convenient. He lived ever by his wits. On this occasion he circled Lake Ontario, found the enemies of the Iroquois, but never brought them to Champlain's help. On the contrary he went with them in the other direction, pleading later that he had been made captive. Almost surely he saw the Ohio River, but unlike his master, Champlain, he was not interested in mere geography. Letting the circumstances determine his career, he turned his back on the Ohio, circled east and became a Susquehannock Indian for the season. With this tribe he moved east on the Susquehanna River, and passed through Pennsylvania and came down to the Bay of the Mother of God, Chesapeake Bay.

There was another "young man" of Champlain's who came nearer to finding the road of the Mississippi than Brulé, and he deserved to come nearer. His name was Nicolet, and it was a name which he kept clear of stain. He passed an apprenticeship of two years with the Algonquins on the road between Montreal and Georgian Bay, yet, though young and adaptable, he remained to the end one of whom Champlain could be proud. It is told of him that once he lived for seven weeks on the barks of trees : an Indian could do the same. But he surpassed the Indians in playing the part among them of a peacemaker. He led an embassy of the Hurons to make peace between that people and the Iroquois, and he made peace and came back alive. For nine years he lived on Lake Nipissing, not ruling the Indians, but influencing them for good, and acting as interpreter and mediator between them and the French.

It was as a peacemaker that Nicolet first entered the lands of the United States. He had been sent by the Hurons of Lake Huron (in Canada) to the tribe called the Stinking People or People of the Sea, on Lake Michigan, at Green Bay where Lake Michigan curves up its back as if to touch Lake Superior. There he sought to make peace between the Hurons and the Stinking People.

"Stinking People !" Nicolet puzzled about that word. He learned that they were so called because they lived in a marsh which smelt like a salt marsh. He came to the conclusion that they did live on a salt sea : the Pacific Ocean, or the Straits of Anian. So he took with him in one of his two canoes, which were manned by seven Indians, an especially fine robe of green damask with birds embroidered on it — a garment in Chinese style. If he came on any Chinamen trading with the Stinkards he would be properly dressed to greet them.

So in 1634, four years after Boston was founded, Nicolet arrived at Wisconsin. He sent two Indians ahead of him, who announced his arrival and assembled for his reception five thousand Indians. Then Nicolet advanced, accoutered in his Chinese silk, and holding in each hand a pistol — not for war but for ceremony. He fired the pistols. At the thunder the women and children fled. The warriors, however, never blinked an eye. Nicolet smoked the peace pipe with them, made peace between them and the Hurons. Then he returned.

Before he returned, Nicolet made a detour which brought him almost to the Mississippi. He went up the

Fox River from Green Bay, towards the headwaters of
the Wisconsin, which flows south into the Mississippi.
He may even have seen the Wisconsin as Brulé may have
seen the Ohio. But he was no more aware of his proximity to the Great Water than he was of his proximity
to the present town of Oshkosh. He returned to the
Ottawa River never knowing what luck was almost his.
To him our country remained but a repetition of rivers
and forests — no particular design to it — stretching from
Quebec to near Tartary.

The next man who came at all near to finding out what
and where was the Great Water, was Father Jogues — or
rather Father Jogues and Father Raymbault, two Jesuits.
It was the Recollect Franciscans who had first come to
Quebec and who as missionaries had begun the missionary
explorations, but they had been succeeded by the Jesuits.
These Jesuits soon acquired an aptitude as explorers by
adopting the habit of accompanying the Indians round
Quebec on their winter hunting-trips, which could not
help being exploring trips. Father Jogues and Raymbault on the other hand set out from Lake Huron, from
Georgian Bay, and they did not go on a hunting-trip.
It was an independent voyage of exploration that they
made, not so much geographical as ethnological, in order
to find out what tribes were their neighbors and what
were the missionary possibilities among them. Also the
tribes of the West had called for them.

It would have been true poetic justice if Father Jogues
had discovered the Mississippi. Father Jogues was twice
martyred for us by the Mohawks on the Mohawk River
in New York State. The first time he came back to life

though maimed. The second time he went safely to Paradise. He is now Saint Isaac Jogues. But even without martyrdom, without canonization, he would have won our hearts by his utter generosity, and by a sweetness wonderfully wedded to fortitude. He was a man whom we would like to honor in every way.

Father Jogues and Raymbault did go farther west than Nicolet. For seventeen days in the summer of 1641 they paddled westward, ever on Lake Huron, along the north shore. Then they came to the rapids rushing toward them from Lake Superior, which they called by the name (of which the spelling if not the pronunciation lasts), of Sault Ste. Marie. Then on they continued for nine days into Lake Superior, and came to the country of the Sioux Indians. To the south lay the source of the Mississippi but they were not giving thought to it. What Saint Isaac Jogues was thinking about was the Indians. Two thousand of them met him at the Sault, and they had never, he said, seen a European nor heard of God. He was preoccupied with them and forgot about the Pacific and the Straits of Anian. It was not reserved for Saint Isaac Jogues to discover the Great River.

Nor was it reserved for Radisson and Groseilliers, who came next, to discover it. They were not saints and they were not Jesuits, although at one time they had worked for the Jesuits. They were bush-rangers, trappers, fur-traders, "*coureurs de bois*," and not very noble ones at that. They had turned traitor to France through spite, and had tried to give the Hudson Bay region to the English. But they were able woodsmen. Love of gain might well have led them to the Great River.

It was ten years after Saint Isaac Jogues' expedition that they did their exploring. Later they wrote a book about what they had seen and phrased it in their own special English and printed it in England in order "to sell" Canada to the English. With such a purpose they did not always tell the truth, and with their absence of geographic training did not always know what the truth was, so it is hard to know exactly where they went but it is safe to say that they visited at least Michigan and Wisconsin.

Some people read their account of their travels for its picturesque description of a trapper's life. They did indeed know such a life, and they described it in an English no one has ever used before or since, like this :

"It is strange thing when victualls are wanting, worke whole nights and dayes, lye downe on the bare ground, and not alwayes that hap, the breech in the water, the feare in the buttocks, to have the belly empty, the weariness in the bones, and drowsiness of the body by the bad weather that you are to suffer, having nothing to keepe you from such calamity."

Michiganers should read it for its description of Michigan. Never has a real-estate agent given such a glowing description of any land :

"We embarked ourselves on the delightfulest lake of the world. I took notice of their cottages and of the journeys of our navigation, for because that the country was so pleasant so beautiful and fruitful that it grieved me to see that the world could not discover more inticing countries to live in. This, I say, because that the Europeans fight for a rock in the sea against one another, or for a steril land and horrid country, that the people sent here, or there, by the changement of the aire engenders sickness and dies thereof. Contrary wise those kingdoms are so delicious and under so temperate a climate, plentiful of all things, the earth bringing forth its fruit twice a year, the people live long and lusty and wise in their way," and so on, but listen to the end : "The further we sejourned the delightfuller the land was to us. I can say that in my life-time I never saw a more incomparable country for all I have been in Italy ; yet Italy comes short of it — "

Yet it is just as well that they did not discover the Mississippi. Big things should not be discovered by such big talkers.

The next Frenchmen who incurred the chance of finding the Mississippi were a mixed exploring party composed of La Salle and two Sulpician priests. For Sulpicians to have discovered the Mississippi would have been very appropriate. They had founded the City of Montreal in a spirit of adventurous missionary enterprise. They were devoted to Our Lady, believed they had come to Canada at her bidding. They had named their mission, which was to become the City of Montreal, Ville-Marie de Montreal. It would have been very happy to have these unearthly men have an earthly success. These particular Sulpicians were moreover men of rare courage and geographic science. One was Father Dollier de Casson, an ex-officer of cavalry who had served with Turenne, and was still but thirty-three years of age. The other, Galinée, was an ex-officer of the French Marine, an excellent navigator, log-keeper and map-maker. As for La Salle, if human energy deserves anything, he deserved a great deal. He was not a priest, not a missionary, and his interest was more in the silver mines of New Spain, to which he hoped to find a road, than in any geographical knowledge. And he was, worse than that, an irascible and occasionally an ill-spirited man, partly because he had started to be a Jesuit and had found he had no vocation, which left him disgruntled with himself and with the Jesuits. Yet he was indomitable. He stood for the great energy of France in the time of Louis XIV. He too would have been a timely discoverer of the Mississippi.

The party started forth from Montreal in 1668, westward. It was able to take the obvious road toward the Mississippi, that is the St. Lawrence River, and then the two lakes, with the Erie River connecting them, of Ontario and Erie, for this was a period of momentary peace between the French and the Iroquois. They passed through the Iroquois towns of New York State and were entertained by the Iroquois and by the Jesuits who were establishing themselves amid the Iroquois. Then they split into two parties : La Salle went southerly, the Sulpicians northerly.

Neither party came to the Mississippi. La Salle would have gladly come to it — it was his dream — and he may have come to the Ohio, which offered him a long but sure path to it, but he really knew not enough about the Indian tongues to know how near he was to his goal. So he turned back. Dollier de Casson and Galinée discovered Niagara Falls, or heard the thunders of its cataracts as they passed from Lake Ontario to Lake Erie.

They also discovered the Sainte Croix River running from Lake Michigan to Lake Erie. They passed by the site (waiting to make automobiles) of Detroit. But they were looking for converts (which they did not find), and not for the Mississippi River, and they went to the Jesuits at Mackinac, but no farther, and they did not discover the Great Water.

And now we come to Joliet. While the Sulpician Fathers were hearing the thunders of Niagara, they came upon a Canadian explorer who was much more than a mere bush-ranger : Monsieur Joliet. He had just returned from an investigation of the copper mines or the signs of copper on Lake Superior. On his way back he had found some Iroquois prisoners about to be put to death by the Ottawas. These prisoners he had ransomed and he was restoring them to their nation. He was a quiet, unassuming man who did things well, and chose to do good things without making much of them. He had once, as had La Salle, planned to be a Jesuit, and then had discovered that he likewise had no Jesuit vocation. But unlike La Salle he was not by the change of his career rendered disgruntled. As La Salle was too irascible, he was perhaps too submissive. His vocation was to explore, and — when it fell across his path — to do such a good deed as the ransoming of the Iroquois. In 1671, Joliet received a commission from Talon, the Intendant of New France, to go, not this time to Lake Superior and the copper mines, but toward the silver mines of Mexico.

This errand was in no wise directly connected with a missionary purpose : its aim was the acquisition of more wealth for a struggling colony which found it hard to

subsist from the profits of the fur-trade. The energy
behind the errand was primarily Talon's, but Talon's energy was really but the energy of Colbert, Louis XIV's
minister of finance, who was bent on making France the
richest nation in the world by giving her a life-blood of
precious metals, and a good health of manufactures and
commerce. Joliet, acting simply as an agent of Colbert,
and energized by France's new economic ambitions,
might have himself come to the Mississippi and floated
down it, down toward New Spain's silver mines. But as
a matter of fact he united himself and his expedition to
the energy of the missionaries : he took with him Father
Marquette, a Jesuit.

Why was this ? Was it that Joliet was used to relying
on Jesuits, having been a candidate for their order ? Was
it simply that he was a man who did not like too much
responsibility, who could rule himself, but not an expedition ? Or was it that he needed a geographer with
him, he being a man of instinct, more of a *coureur de bois*
than a scientist ? Or was it that Talon, though not always too friendly to the Jesuits, realized well their ability and their geographical learning ? They had an institute of geography at Quebec. They had records.
They were a clearing-house of information. Perhaps he
had been discussing the affair of the Great River with
Father Mercier, the Superior of the Jesuits in New
France, and had heard from him that there was a Jesuit
who had been on the south shores of Lake Superior, and
who knew also the regions of the Stinking People, and
who was begging to go to the Great River concerning
which he professed to have accurate information.

All we know is that on December 8th, 1672, the Feast of the Immaculate Conception, Joliet with six other Frenchmen arrived at the mission of Saint Ignatius on the north shore of the Straits of Mackinac, which connect Lakes Huron and Michigan, and presented to Father Marquette in the name of Talon, and of his Jesuit superior, the opportunity to go in search of the Great River. Jesuits have to have a liking of cheerful obedience, but in this case Father Marquette had to make no effort in order to be cheerful at the errand proffered him. Born at Laon in northern France in that antique Frankish acropolis, which lone and watch-tower-like looks down upon the plain of Champagne spread about it as a map, he had himself since childhood looked forth with the eyes of a geographer on the world about him. But also to the east of Laon, in the plain, discernible to his eye was the miracle-working shrine of Notre Dame de Liesse — Our Lady of holy hidden merciful mystical mirth. — He had dreamed, therefore, of being such a geographer as would make the whole world filled with that *Liesse*, in other words a missionary in far lands. He had become a Jesuit in order to pursue that calling. By effort or aptitude he had prepared himself well to be such a missionary, for he had acquired a facility in the learning of strange languages, and a familiarity with the latest information brought in by world-explorers.

Father Marquette had crossed the ocean to New France in 1666, when he was but twenty-nine, and at Three Rivers, under one of the ablest of the Jesuits, Father Druillettes, he had learned some seven Indian languages. Yet even then, even with all his zeal, and all his hardihood, he had not enjoyed great success as a missionary. At La Pointe, the mission of the Holy Ghost in Wisconsin, at the end of the world, he had ministered to a gathering of refugee Hurons and Ottawas. The Hurons seemed to be falling back rather than marching ahead as Christians; the Ottawas there were a positive scandal.

The only earthly thing that gave him heart was the friendliness of various tribes of the Illinois Indians, who kept inviting him south, telling him of their country, and boasting of its Great River, or Great Water. They also told him of people to the south, White Men, who gave to the Indians prayer beads, and who had prayer-bells (the news of which had there trickled northward to the Great Lakes), in other words of the Spanish. But he had no liberty to follow this prospect: his post was with the Hurons and the Ottawas, with his own failure. He stayed on with them in Wisconsin till the Sioux drove them out, and then retreated east with them to St. Ignatius Mission at Mackinac, where he continued, unfretful but quite aware of the little harvest he was reaping, to hope that the Illinois might be those to whom he might some day be sent. With them he could start anew. And now Joliet arrived. He, the youngest of the Jesuits at St. Ignatius, had been singled out for an adventure which in his humility he had dared only indirectly to pray for. Possibly now with his rare talent for languages and his skill in navigating rivers he might find the success of which he could not help dreaming.

All winter long he had to wait for the season to travel. He had to stare at the white snowdrifts, the black pine-trees that bristle at Mackinac, and at the cold black-blue waters of Michigan and Huron. Not till as late as May 17th, 1673, could traveling be begun. Then he, the man of intellect who had the map of the world in his mind and Joliet, the man of instinct who had the forests and lakes of Canada and the northern New World ever in his eye, started through Lake Michigan toward the oft-mentioned region of Oshkosh, the country of the Stinking People, Green Bay. Into Green Bay they turned and they penetrated the Fox River. They were seven Frenchmen in two birch-bark canoes.

They came to a waterfall, twelve feet high. Around it they carried their canoes. Then the waters spread out to a lake, Lake Winnebago. There was nothing new in this. Other Jesuits and Nicolet had been here before. It was merely an old Jesuit road.

Next they came to a swamp, which was a barrier only because it presented a thousand paths instead of one. But here Father Marquette's affability with the Indians and his knowledge of their languages helped him. Two Indians were persuaded to show them the path to another river, the Wisconsin, which they planned to follow toward the Great Water. So knowing were the Indians that after having waded for merely two thousand seven hundred paces they came to a southward-flowing current: the Wisconsin. On the seventeenth of June — how very simple — only a month from St. Ignatius, the current carried them into the Great River. It looked like a Great River, but, more than that, Father Marquette as a geographer knew it to be the Great River. Father Marquette felt a joy that he could not express — *"une*

joie que je ne peux pas expliquer." As for Joliet, I suspect he took the floating into the river as a matter of
course. It was one more stream. He was busy with his
paddle, with his piloting, with thoughts of a next camp.

If Father Marquette had merely entered the Mississippi
he would have done nothing extraordinary. The Mississippi was to Spaniards a known river. It was the River
of the Holy Spirit on their maps. Its mouth was ascer-
tained. In 1520 it had been first marked by mariners
and De Soto had crossed it in 1540. And a year later his
men had floated down several hundred miles of it.
Neither Father Marquette nor Joliet were the first dis-
coverers of its waters : they were more than a hundred
years late. What they did discover was its importance
as a road. They discovered that the entire interior of
our country belongs to it, that it cuts our country in half,
drawing a line from Canada to the Gulf of Mexico.
They discovered what the mysterious Great Water really
was.

They could not help appreciating as they canoed down
its vastness the vastness of our continent which enclosed
and fed it, for they passed the formidable roar where the
Missouri poured its muddy waters into their path to
make their path doubly great. An impetuosity "of large
and entire trees, branches and floating islands" came rushing from the northwest into the Mississippi out of this
Pekinanoui, or Muddy River — out of this Missouri. The
geographer in Father Marquette added to the world's
map a large region to the northwest which filled up then
and there once and for all in his mind the Straits of
Anian. He made new plans for his life : he would visit

the region.   What innumerable tribes sitting in darkness must be waiting for him there !

On he went — on they went.   They rode in hollowed trees now instead of birch-bark canoes, because of the snags which would tear birch-bark as a stag's antlers would tear paper.   They passed cities invisible, yet to be built.   They passed the great mouth of the Wabash. They passed the city which was to consider itself as on the New World's Nile : Memphis, Tennessee.   They came to where the Arkansas River comes in from the west.   But this was far enough.   Father Marquette had discovered that the river which Talon had hoped would flow into the Gulf of California was none other than the River of the Holy Spirit of the Spanish maps, and that it was headed for the Gulf of Mexico.   If he continued on it he might soon be among Spaniards, and his companions, if not he, might be there be treated not with entire hospitality by Spain.   And every mile he moved made the return road up-river homeward longer.   So about he turned at the thirty-second degree of latitude.   He had accomplished his task, he had cooperated with Joliet for the glory of France.   Now for his more important business dedicated more directly to the glory of God — the conversion of the Illinois.

Father Marquette had had greatness thrust upon him, a kind of greatness that he had never aspired to.   He became of all the French explorers the privileged explorer : the one man who had discovered what the others had been consciously and unconsciously looking for.   It might be said that he was not enough greater than the other Jesuits or other Sulpicians or other "bush-rangers"

or other La Salles, to have this honor thrust upon him.
Perhaps not, and since when did all honors seem to be
poetically just ?

But this there is to be noted : he was to the point of
superstition devoted to the Immaculate Conception of
Our Lady. To be unique in this respect among the
Jesuits was indeed to be unique, for all the unbelievers
can break their ribs with laughter at the devotion of the
Jesuits of New France to the tremendous purity of Our
Lady. It was their safety, their hope. But Father Marquette was nevertheless in his uniqueness great. Even
before he had a will to be devoted to her, he had been
captured by her. Since he had been nine he had fasted
Saturdays in her honor. And in his later youth he had
invented a special series of prayers which he called the
"Crown of the Immaculate Conception," which he daily
recited. In the center of this crown, like a jewel set in
it, was a cluster of ejaculations repeated four times :

"Ave filia dei patris, ave mater filii dei, ave sponsa
spiritus sancti, ave templum totius trinitatis, pcr sanctam
virginitatem et immaculatam conceptionem tuam, puris-
sima virgo, emunda cor et carnem meam. — Hail daughter
of God the Father, hail Mother of God the Son, hail
spouse of the Holy Ghost, hail temple of all the Persons
of the Trinity, by your holy virginity and your Immaculate Conception, make clean my heart and my body."

He had but one obsessing idea : the Immaculate Conception. Every deed and day of his life was important
or unimportant in terms of its relation to that subject of
all his song.

It was on December 8th, the Feast in celebration of that

Sinlessness, that he had received his order to go toward the Great Water, and he did not take the date as a mere coincidence. As soon as he had floated from the Wisconsin into the Mississippi, "we began," he said, "all together a new devotion to the Blessed Virgin Immaculate which we practised daily, addressing to her special prayers to place under her protection both our persons and the success of our voyage."

Father Marquette as he continued down the river which inscribes itself like an heraldic tree on the shield of our country's shape, which is, as it were, the device on our shield, gave it the name which symbolized to him more than any other name God's bounty to human beings ; he called it the River of the Immaculate Conception.

CHAPTER V

THE FRENCH BUBBLE

BEFORE the voyage of Father Marquette and Monsieur Joliet down the Mississippi, the lands of the United States had been of but little concern to France. After that they became the seat of a French project so sudden in its appearance, so grand and glittering is its amplitude, so once again sudden in its disappearance that it can be called a bubble — the French Bubble.

The French Bubble was but one single bubble, one single plan of hopefulness, one single speculation. The project of the French was to build a France in the New World as Spain had built a Spain in the New World. So to do might involve an appropriation of certain portions of North America which on the map were marked Spanish, but which Spain could be held to have forfeited by not having occupied them. It would almost surely involve an ousting of the thriving English squatters from their control of the Atlantic seaboard, or at least their subjugation. Were the project to be achieved, it would lead to the creation of a French North America extending from the Arctic Circle, where human habitation ended, to beyond the southern borders of our country where Spanish habitation solidly began. This enterprise had its religious aspect, for France was at this time a very believing country and its King considered himself a champion — even *the* champion — of the Catholic Church.

It also had its financial aspect, for France was now trying to be as rich as Spain had once been rich, though by a different method. It also had its military aspect, for France needed the power of arms to protect herself against other nations and to lead her life. But the aspects were all aspects of but one bubble.

It is well, however, to take up the various aspects of France's religious, financial and military speculation as if they were separate speculations, separate bubbles. It happens that the word bubble — through sad experience — has in the modern world been associated mainly with financial speculation, and we can begin with the financial aspect.

By the voyage of Father Marquette and the subsequent voyages of La Salle, France became virtual proprietor of our entire Mississippi Valley. Spain, with an infant and imbecile king, was in no position to assert her prior right to the region. The English of England were interested only in the Atlantic seacoast of America. The English of the New World looked either back to England or to the southeast. France therefore could count herself as unchallenged owner of the Mississippi and all its tributaries, and could make plans accordingly. And when we look back at what she was laying claim to without dispute, we cannot help thinking that her highest hopes were justified. She owned a great V of land which had its point at the mouth of the Great River and its one arm extending to the Rockies in Montana, and its other extending to Lake Ontario. Within that embrace nature had prepared millions of acres fabulously fertile for wheat, which were levelled already for the plow, and did not need to be cleared of rocks and trees, and there were the specially prepared grazing lands of the interminable plains, and there was scarcely a corner of the region that was uninhabitable or inaccessible. It was all of it a land made by and blessed by the Mississippi and its benificent arms. And then, as if to overwhelm with its generosity, it had ready to present to its owners the coal and iron of Pennsylvania, and Lake Superior's copper. It had in the old days also the wealth of furs. It was moreover accessible to Europe, the St. Lawrence providing one way into it and the lower Mississippi the other. And it was accessible only to the French, for they owned the two entrances. France was not credulous in seeing in this new possession a possibility of immense enrichment. She gave the name of Colbert, her minister of finance, to the Mississippi. She gave the name of the richest king in Europe, Louis XIV, her King, to the regions about the River Colbert; she called the northern part of the V Upper Louisiana, the southern part Lower Louisiana.

It cannot be said, however, that France based her hopes on what we see she might have based them on. She did little talking about agriculture, none about cattle. Her opportunities in the fur-trade were greatly enhanced by the taking over of the Mississippi Valley, for not only had she gained access to new supplies of fur, but she was in a position to bar the English and Dutch from such an access. Yet she did not lose her head thinking of furs. Such a source of wealth had become so well known that it appealed little to the imagination. It had become a definite trade with definite profits, and definite hazards, with a huge yet limited and known-to-be-limited market. But mines did appeal to the imagination as mines always do, for they tantalize by their hiddenness. They have the charm and risk of a lottery. France dreamed of mines in Louisiana and he who dreams of mines has limitless dreams. Copper had been discovered on Lake Superior by the Jesuits before Father Marquette made his southern journey. And soon after the journey lead was discovered. And why not silver next and why not gold ? France at this time was stifling her imagination at home. She sent it to Louisiana there to disport.

It was with hopes of great financial profit that New Orleans was founded in 1717. A stock company, like the English stock companies which founded Jamestown, Boston, Charleston, was entrusted with Lower Louisiana. That the stock company did not flourish made no difference to the hopefulness of France. A true sense of the ultimate wealth of the Mississippi Valley gave Frenchmen a false sense concerning its immediate returns. Louisiana stood for limitless potentiality, and as such it became woven into the credit system of France. John Law, who tried to give to France the equivalent of a Bank of Amsterdam or a Bank of England, used the name of the Mississippi, and more than the name of it, as the warrant of his Royal Bank's inexhaustible soundness. He therefore lent the Mississippi's name to the great bubble which wrecked so many Frenchmen : The Mississippi Bubble.

John Law was a Scotchman who was born in Edinburgh in the very year when Father Marquette heard that he was to go southward to the Mississippi, but that

is no reason why he should have ever had anything to do
with the Mississippi.   It was one of the most unpredicta-
ble things in history that this Scotchman should ever
have had anything to do with France at all, that France's
destiny should have been held for a time in his hand.
And yet we can see how it came about.   It was not mere
chance.

Law was, as I say, a Scotchman, and being a Scotchman, he thought about money, but also being a Scotchman
he had much more of a mathematical mind than most
Englishmen — and certainly than most English bankers.
He thought about money and about banking mathematically, as Descartes thought about life mathematically,
as Sir Isaac Newton thought about the stars mathematically.   He was not a swindler.   He was a philosopher — a scientist.   Instead of studying the circulation of
the stars, however, he studied the circulation of money,
and thought that he had found the secret of moving
money as Sir Isaac Newton found the secret of falling
bodies.

Such a man was well-calculated to be of interest to
France.   The French monarchy had not handed over its
powers to a bank.   It was suspicious of banks, and recognized that the Bank of England had changed the English
monarchs into mere pensioners.   Yet the benefits conferred by the Bank of England and the Bank of Amsterdam in the way of stimulating commerce and industry
were obvious — painfully obvious.   For after the death
of Louis XIV, France was in desperate financial straits,
whereas England and Holland were not.   It needed
bankers with their common sense, yet did not want

bankers with their all-too-common sense. A mathematician who could really rationalize about banking systems was what would much please the intellectual French.

Jessamy John, as Law was called, was the man for France, but Jessamy John would never have found his way into France or into the French court if he had not really been Jessamy John. He was a lady's man, handsome, duel-fighting, who had had to flee his own country for a duel. He was more than a cloistered philosopher : there was a bit of the adventurer about him. He had manners that could attract attention ; he had a presence that opened doors to him.

It was in 1715 that Louis XIV, the King with the greatest national income in Europe, had died. He had become immeshed in wars, the cost of which had drained his coffers. He had had to borrow from the moneyed ; he had left a debt of a hundred and forty-two million pounds sterling. In the uncertainty of it commerce was paralyzed. Money disappeared from circulation. And the new king, little great-grandson Louis XV, was but a boy ; and a Regent was governing. And everything was in a bad way. Yet France was at the same time rich in fields, rich in industry, rich in diligence and every skill. It seemed as if something very simple was all that was needed, some bit of advice. And the philosopher, Jessamy John, was at the door, dressed like a dandy, dressed for entrance, quite capable of giving mathematical advice with an engaging gesture.

Law had the advice. National prosperity, he said, was due to the plentifulness of a circulating medium of exchange : money. Such money could best be paper money issued by a bank of which the credit could be unchallengeable. It was all very simple. All that he had to do was to find the unchallengeable credit. Leave that to him. He would arrange it.

And he did arrange it. Within a few years he was Comptroller General of the Finances of France, and head of a bank which had first been his bank and then had become France's Royal Bank. He issued a currency of three billion paper pounds whose value was based on the return from France's taxes and from the profits of various over-seas trading companies, one of which was the Company of the West which had founded New Orleans and was identified with Louisiana's riches. The credit was indeed unchallengeable — so unchallengeable that the bank-notes were more precious than gold, and forced gold out of circulation. Those who owned gold did not know what to do with it. They started to cart it to Holland till royal decree stopped them.

And how the shares in Law's bank soared in value! There were 600,000 shares of this bank, but most of them were owned by the Regent; only 200,000 were in the hands of the public. Over these few 200,000 shares there rose the most incredible and picturesque speculation. Not only the rich bought and sold them, but the poor, and not only the French but foreigners — even the King of England. Three hundred thousand foreigners flocked to Paris in November 1719, to grow rich trading in the shares. There was no stock-exchange; the street Quinquempoix near the bank was first used by those who wished to buy and sell. Lucky men who owned lodgings on that street made fortunes over night. A cobbler fitted his shop with chairs like a grandstand and received two hundred French pounds — say one hundred of our dollars — a day by renting them. When the jostling in the street made it impossible to conduct the transactions in such narrow quarters, another place was sought. Only the Place Vendôme would do. Endless were the comic tales of the fortunes made. The shares went up to sixty times their original value. One foreigner, an Englishman, a noble, by name Gage, made so much money that he offered to buy the throne of Poland from Poland's King: price offered, five million pounds. But he was no madder than the rest.

It is not necessary to tell what happened; we have grown used to such things and we know. Yet it should be said for the benefit of Law that he did not steal, nor did he trick anybody. It was simply that his algebra had not taken into account human nature. The success of the money-making bank killed it. Some human beings strangely enough had become satisfied with their gains, and not because they doubted the worth of the paper money, but because they had made enough, were glad to be out of the affair. They handed in their paper to the Bank and took out gold. When an edict forbade the keeping of gold — not more than five hundred French pounds in a family — the gold began to be hidden or exported. Finally the confidence of the public was gone; everything tumbled. And all those that lost and all those who had gained were called Mississippians.

A year later a French priest, Charlevoix, was commissioned by the French government to investigate this Mississippi concerning which there had been such extraordinary financial planning. He took the waterways from Canada to Louisiana, using Chicago as his river junction, and descending the Illinois to the Mississippi. He went down the Mississippi. He met various Indian tribes which, thanks to the peace-making efforts of the missionaries and the generally fair methods of the French traders, treated him well. But he saw no evidence of a financial exploitation of the country. Except for an occasional abandoned warehouse he saw no evidence of any financial crash. It was like an empty country. He went a thousand miles without seeing a white man.

Then he came to New Orleans. That was at least something, and if it excited his derision it was not because it was small and puny and disordered as all pioneer settlements are, but because it contrasted so with the accounts of it in the prospectuses which he had read. In his letter home he refers to the "eight hundred fine houses and five parishes which our *Mercure* bestowed on it two years ago," and professes to be surprised that they have now dwindled to one hundred shacks "placed in no very good order ; to a large warehouse built of timber ; to two or three houses which would be no ornament to a village in France," and finally to a miserable extra warehouse which he says served for a chapel till the chapel had to be removed to a tent.

As a financial bubble Louisiana burst very soon. It was so huge, so distended that it burst into almost nothing.

The military bubble lasted much longer. In 1672 Talon from Canada had written to his master Colbert : "This part of the French monarchy is destined to a grand future. All that I see around me points to it ; and the colonies of foreign nations [he was thinking mostly of the English, but he linked all foreigners together as outsiders] so long settled on the sea-board, are trembling with fright in view of what his Majesty has accomplished here within the last seven years. The measures we have taken to confine them within narrow limits, and the prior claim we have established against them by formal acts of possession, do not permit them to extend themselves except at peril of having war declared against them as usurpers ; and this, in fact, is what they seem greatly to fear."

France had the confidence in herself in the 1680's that a nation used to military victories acquires. In 1689 she decided to cripple the English forever in the New World by depriving them of New York City. New York City was not at that time a rich booty. The English governor at this time describes its worth to England's King in a manner that gives little idea of its future importance.

"New York is the metropolis, is scituate upon a barren island bounded by Hudson's River and the East River that runs into the sound, and hath nothing to support it but trade which chiefly flows from Flower and bread they make of the Corne the west end of Long Island and Qopas produceth ; and which is sent to the West Indies, and there is brought in returne from thence among other things a liquor called Rumm, the duty whereof considerably increaseth your Majesty's revenue."

But the French thought in military terms. New York State — the Hudson River and the Mohawk — was the road round the Alleghanies west to Chicago ; it was the one such road for the English colonies. Should New

York City be taken from the English, then the English would lose this road. They would be hemmed in from access to the fur-trade save over the mountains. And what is more, they could not attack the French in Canada for they would have lost the road of the Hudson River. And finally, with New York City fallen to the French, the English colonies would be separated into two groups which could not again act in concert.

The French did not capture New York in 1689. All they did was to capture somewhat bloodily, in the dead of winter, Schenectady, which they burned. The truth is they had not in the settlements of Canada, which were largely missionary and spiritual foundations, enough men for any operation of proper military grandeur. New York persisted as English. New York grew.

And soon the tables were turned on France. Louisiana became on the defensive, and Canada too, for the English wanted the fur-trade, and they wanted to expand westerly.

In 1743 it was the Governor of New York — Governor Clark — who was proposing to be the aggressor. "I have often reflected," he wrote, "on the progress of our natural enemies, the French, who have made in their settlements on the back of us, chiefly since the Peace of Utrecht (1713), the vast increase of their Indian trade, the interruption of ours by the power which their communications between Canada and Mississippi (by means of Lake Cadaraqui or Ontario) gives to them over all the Indian Nations." But Governor Clark did more than reflect. Even though there was at the instant no war he had a suggestion: "I propose that a regiment of eight hundred men be sent from England — with an engineer, Artillery and Ammunition, and posted in the Seneca's country on the Lake Cadaraqui, — that the harbor be fortified and barracks erected for the men." He wished to attack the forts which the French had been building to protect their domain of the Mississippi Valley. He was going to profit by the fact that Louis XIV had never captured New York, that the western road was still open.

New York fretted at France's ownership of the Mississippi Valley because of commercial jealousy. Farther south the colonists fretted at it for a reason even more cogent. Virginia had a population by this time of a quarter of a million, and the other States of Maryland, Pennsylvania, the Carolinas, had enough population at least to have a land hunger. Colonists were eager to cross the Alleghanies and settle in the region of the western rivers. In 1748, Thomas Lee and twelve others, including Lawrence and Augustine, brothers of George Washington, and Joe Wantary, a Quaker merchant of London, had received a grant of 500,000 acres in the region of the Ohio River, western Pennsylvania. They were stockholders in the Ohio Company which had various privileges but one important obligation which was not a spiritual one such as French and Spanish kings imposed on their subjects : they were obliged within seven years to settle in the Ohio region one hundred families at least, and to build a fort, and to maintain a garrison. How could they fulfill the obligation ? France in her solicitude for her communications between Canada and Louisiana, and in preparation for the future development of the region concerning which she continued to have lordly, if patient, prospects, would not allow the English into the Ohio's region. She claimed it as her own, and built forts there. It was the rampart of her future wealth. She would not be ousted, as Spain had been ousted, by a failure to occupy.

In 1755, an English army landed in Virginia to march up the Potomac through the forests of the Alleghanies and pierce these ramparts of a realm which though it existed, existed but in hope. As the financial bubble of the Mississippi had been pricked, so let the military bubble be pricked.

This army was Braddock's army. It was twenty-two hundred in strength and had six hundred pack horses, besides the artillery horses. The camp was half as populous as the only real city in the great Louisiana to the west, New Orleans. It was twice as populous as all Upper Louisiana — if we do not count the Indians in it. It marched from a seacoast crowded with two million inhabitants. How could such a force be withstood?

Yet the military planning of the French still held good. There was in the Ohio region a French fort, Fort Duquesne, at the confluence of two westward-flowing rivers — the Monongahela and the Ohio. The fort itself was of little account, not against the artillery of Braddock; nor was it garrisoned to support a siege. There were in it two companies of French regulars, less than two hundred Canadians, and around it hovered a more or less reliable force of eight hundred Indian allies. But the French were not foolish enough to imprison themselves in their fort. They went forth, about nine hundred in all (counting Indians), to await the English in the habitat which the French had made so much their own, the forest. The English never saw the army against them, not more, they said, than a hundred men of it. But they saw the forest and soon the forest began to crackle with gunfire. And the English cannon could not mow down the trees, and the well-drilled soldiers could not charge the June foliage. The army ended by fleeing, and by burning its hundred wagons of transport in a bonfire of triumph. The military bubble still continued.

But soon even that came to an end. Three years later, in September when the St. Lawrence River was beginning to smoke in the cold nights, an English force was able to land on the heights above the fortress of Quebec — the fortress from which all the explorers had set forth which had brought Louisiana into being. Because of Louisiana, that fortress had to be attacked. And it fell. And when it fell there was no use doing any more planning for Louisiana; the gate which made Louisiana worth planning for had fallen. In 1763, France ceded Canada to England, and with it, without too many sighs, all of Louisiana, all of it east of the Mississippi, the rest of it going to Spain.

Thus all the brilliant French victories within our borders went for nothing. They entered history books and became legends. Their one lasting consequence was the hardening of the English colonists so that they would be able to fight their mother-country, England. So far as France was concerned, the military project of Louisiana was a bubble of heroic duration, but in the end only a bubble and a costly one at that.

Now for the more religious aspect of France's project

in our land, for what she did to establish a Christendom under the French flag as the Pope had originally commissioned the Spaniards to establish it under a Spanish flag, for the effort she made to rule over a region composed of Indians owing allegiance to the King of France and of French colonists, living fellow-Christians with the Indians!

Long before France had a commercial or military interest in our country, long before Father Marquette had floated down the Mississippi and made our lands seem important to the great world-power of Louis XIV's France — even in 1611 — the Marquise de Guercheville, a pious lady who had a scorn for the merely secular aspects of life, sent to Mt. Desert Island in our Maine, a French colony which was to be above all a colony of specifically Christian France — of the France dedicated to Our Lady. It was to be a colony, but also, and principally, a Jesuit mission. If we except the Huguenots under Ribaut in Florida, who can easily be excepted because they were less a French colony than an anti-Spanish pirate outpost, this colony was France's first real colony in the United States.

It did not last long. Argall from English Jamestown captured it before it could reap its first crops. He claimed that the colony had planted itself on English land, but he was in motive and training and disposition a corsair, and as such he acted, and as such he treated the French, though he did not make them all walk the plank, and only cast a dozen of the more helpless of them with one priest adrift in an open boat. Argall destroyed a very unworldly colony in a manner very worldly, and he destroyed it with extraordinary promptitude. But the mission on Mt. Desert Island lasted just long enough to stand as a symbol for the spiritual nature of France's first endeavors in our midst.   For the next sixty years the only occupation of our country by the French was a missionary occupation.   It came not directly from France but indirectly from France through Canada, which was itself a missionary foundation, that spiritualized all that came through it.   These emanations from Canada were the very quintessence of missionary effort.   They were missions sent out by a mission.   They belonged scarcely to temporal France at all, and were referred to in the title of the Governor of New France as "other northern regions." The civil and military administration had nothing to do with them, and knew little of their whereabouts. They were Our Lady's outposts rather than Louis XIV's.

There were a score or more of these outposts in the United States, established before the arrival of Marquette.   In 1863 a stone was discovered near the mouth of the Penobscot River in Maine.   On it was written : "On the 8th of June, 1648, I, Friar Leo of Paris, Capuchin missionary, laid this cornerstone of Our Lady of Holy Hope."   At the very same period there was a Jesuit mission among the Abenakis on the Kennebec River in Maine.   During the next twenty years there flourished off and on a dozen Jesuit missions among the Iroquois of New York State.   And there was St. Ignatius's mission — also Jesuit — at the head of Lake Michigan.   And there were Jesuit missions at Sault Ste. Marie and at La Pointe, Wisconsin, and at St. Francis Xavier on Green Bay.   Not all of these missions were named after Our Lady, not a half of them even, but if any one doubts as to whom they were especially dedicated, he has only to read what the world would call the superstitious observations of the Jesuits concerning these missions. Father Chaumonot who first established a mission among the Onondagas had vowed at Our Lady's shrine at Loretto always to do the hardest, most heroic thing with her help. He was utterly hers. His chapel amid the Onondagas was Our Lady's chapel. And Father Bruyas who began the missions among the Mohawks ascribed his only success to a statue of Notre Dame de Foye which he had brought down to Albany from Quebec. Our Lady was becoming France's Conquistadora.

It would not be well to underestimate these early French missions in our midst. The little chapel built on Penobscot Bay by Friar Leo did not last long, for a ship of Cromwell's came by, demolished it, and carried away the missionary founder of it. But there were other Capuchins who continued in Maine. And concerning the beneficence of the work of the Jesuits on the Kennebec we have very happy testimony. Near the Abenaki village where lived the Jesuit there stood a trading post of the Plymouth English Colony. Its agent was John Winslow. Father Druillettes, the Jesuit who evangelized these Indians, did him the offense of spelling his name Ouinslow, but struck up a friendship with him based on sympathy and gratitude. In turn he won Winslow's esteem, and was taken by Winslow on one occasion to Boston at Winslow's expense. But more important for us he admired what Druillettes did for the Indians. Instead of trying to wean the Indians from a Catholic priest, he recommended him to the Indians : "I love and respect the patriarch ; I will lodge him at my house, and will treat him as my brother, for I know very well the good that he does among you, and the life which he there leads."

We have other even more significant testimony to the lasting value of the Jesuits' efforts as among the Abenakis. Today the Abenakis are still Catholic. There was a time when they had to suffer for their faith. After the peace of Utrecht in 1713, France gave up any claim to their lands, and ceded what rights it had to them to the English. The English colonists of Massachusetts did not like the Abenakis' continuing to entertain in their midst a Catholic priest. They attacked the Abenaki village twice and twice burned it, and the last time they killed the priest, Father Râle, Jesuit. After that, the Abenakis were without a priest for eighty years, but even without priest they were not without faith. They used to go three hundred miles to Quebec for confession. They withstood every bribe, every ruse to make them give up their Catholic allegiance and become Protestants. Their perseverance entitles them to admiration, but it also entitles the early Jesuits to the same thing.

The missions of the Jesuits in New York State among the Iroquois had a different climax : their sufficient justification is and will remain Catherine Tekakwitha, an astounding example of Indian heroic virtue. She, as we all know, is now a candidate for canonization, and the only American Indian of our country who has ever been candidate for such an honor. Whether or not she is canonized, she remains an example of what a Christian Indian touched by grace could achieve, such as can awe our entire nation into attention. It was, we presume, the blood of three Christian martyrs, Saint Isaac Jogues, Saint René Goupil, and Saint Jean Lalande — all of whom suffered and died in her village — that brought down such graces upon her. But also the graces were channelled toward her by the establishment in her village of a Jesuit mission, the mission of the martyrs, the little chapel of St. Peter, in which she was baptized, and from which she was guided toward sanctity. The ten Jesuit missions of New York State do not need to plead that they amounted to something. They have only to point to Catherine. What have all our sky-scraping busy cities ever produced like to her?

The Jesuit missions farther west in our land had a success less easy to gauge. The Sulpician Fathers — Dollier de Casson and Galinée — were not impressed by the sanctity or perseverance of the Indians at Mackinac when they visited the mission in 1668. Nor was Father Marquette elated over what had been accomplished in the way of conversions at the three western mission posts, La Pointe, Sault Ste. Marie or St. Francis Xavier. But suppose the missions had not existed, suppose the peace that was diffused from them had not been diffused. Suppose that the Indians of that region had only encountered as White Men brandy-selling fur-traders, does any one imagine that France would have ever descended into the Mississippi Valley at all? Or if she had, would her entry not have been attended by a warfare that never occurred?

After the finding by Father Marquette of the road from Canada to the Gulf these enterprises of the missionaries in our territory became eclipsed by other enterprises far more ambitious.   Who could think of the Mississippi Valley as a place of missionaries when it became the glamorous keystone of France's financial edifice ? And why talk of the forests south of the Saint Lawrence as the dwelling-place of a Catherine Tekakwitha, when they were the field of the victories so much more visible and resounding of Montcalm.   But the missionary effort did not fade out, it redoubled.   True, it had to shift its seat.   In the fierce quarrel that ensued between the English and the French the missionaries nearest the English colonists had to suffer.   After all, the English could scarcely help looking on the missionaries as their enemies, for the missionaries were French, and the French at this time in common parlance were referred to regularly by the English as "our natural enemies."   And the missionaries could scarcely help favoring the side of France, for France was their fatherland and their protector.   So the missions in New York State among the Iroquois had to be abandoned.   And also those in what is now the State of Maine came to an end.   But missionary effort was simply concentrated farther west, on the Great Lakes and in the Mississippi Valley.   And into these regions from the north came the Jesuits and the priests from the Montreal Seminary of Foreign Missions ; and up from the South came too the Jesuits from the Gulf, and the Franciscan Capuchins also.   And also to New Orleans came the Ursuline Sisters, to teach the children of the colonists. It never occurred to France simply to make of Louisiana a financial venture or a military station.   The traders themselves paid for the voyage out of the Ursulines, and the soldiers, of whom there were few, expected their chaplain. And the King of France felt it his royal duty to see that his white colonists and his red subjects of the forests and plains be supplied with priests.

And what came of it all?

Much less than Father Marquette dreamed. The great day in his life had not been the finding of the Mississippi, but the visiting of the Illinois tribe, which had invited him southward, and for the salvation of which he had been glad to make his southward exploration. His great day came the year after his voyage with Joliet. It was the day when he founded a mission, and saw in it every promise of success. This mission of his was on the Illinois River, and he called it, as you may guess, the Mission of the Immaculate Conception. It was the day of his heart, the day which cracked his heart with joy and gave him a foretaste of the Heaven he was during the next winter to enter. A Jesuit who was there gives us an account of Father Marquette's great day:

"Then the father — having directed them to stretch out upon lines several pieces of Chinese taffeta, attached to these four large pictures of the Blessed Virgin, which were visible on all sides. The audience was composed of 500 chiefs and elders, seated in a circle round the father, and of all the young men, who remained standing. They numbered more than 1500 men, without counting the women and children, who are always numerous — the village being composed of five or six hundred fires. The father addressed the whole body of people, and conveyed to them ten messages, by means of ten presents which he gave them. . ."

Father Marquette's mission did have an aftermath.

Twice it moved southward as the Illinois tribe of the Kaskaskias migrated to a new village site, but it persisted, and in 1711 a French naval ensign, visiting it to punish some trappers who were scandalizing the Indians, wrote an account of it.   He was the same ensign who had written concerning the Apalache Indians at Biloxi, his name Pénicaut.   Once again he was surprised by the signs of Christian life among savages.   "The Illinois Kaskaskias are assiduous and adroit in cultivating the land ; they furrow it with a plough, which is not done elsewhere in the lower Mississippi region.   It is the reverend Jesuit fathers who have taught them this. . . They have in their fields a goodly supply of cattle, like oxen and cows.   They have also poultry of all kinds.   They have near to their village three mills to grind their grain ; a wind-mill which belongs to the reverend Jesuit fathers, which is much used by the inhabitants, and two others which are turned by horses which the Illinois Indians are owners of."

Then he describes something of the religious life of the mission : "The great majority of the Illinois are Catholic Christians.   They have a very large church in their village, where there is a baptismal font.   This church is very clean inside ; there are three chapels, the great one in the choir, and two others, one on either side.   They have a belfry with a bell ; they attend regularly High Mass and Vespers.   The Jesuit fathers have translated the psalms and hymns for them into their language.   Both at Mass and at Vespers they chant alternately a verse with the French who live among them.   For example, the Illinois chant a verse of a psalm or hymn in their language, and the French follow with a verse in Latin, to the tune that they use in Europe. For their marriages the banns are announced on three consecutive Sundays or consecutive feasts, and the marriage is performed at Mass, as is done in France."

No other mission of the Mississippi compared with that of the Kaskaskias and even that was to have a doom that would have broken Father Marquette's heart, not with joy, but with sorrow, had he been able to foresee it. Not the Indians, but the French themselves destroyed the mission. In 1763 the Jesuits were suppressed in France, and those who carried out the suppression in Louisiana carried it out with sacrilege. At Kaskaskia the chapel was sacked and its furnishings auctioned. "After the sacred vessels and the vestments had been taken away" — and here I slide into the words of an onlooker who records it — "the shelves of the altar had been thrown down; the linings of the altar had been given to negresses noted for their evil lives; and a large crucifix, which had stood above the altar, and the chandeliers, were found placed in a house whose reputation was not good."

But why go on with what is so painful? The truth is that Kaskaskia's lot was a much happier lot while it lasted than any other French mission in the Mississippi Valley. It was not that there were not elsewhere brave, pious, devoted priests, who were willing to give their lives for the salvation of the Indians. Two priests of the Seminary of Foreign Missions died martyrs' deaths in Lower Louisiana before New Orleans was even founded. And three Jesuits gave up their lives similarly with equal heroism and cheerfulness. And there was tireless enterprise in the missionaries. Distances were nothing to them.

There were never more than twenty French missionaries in the Mississippi Valley (not counting the priests who did parish work with the colonists), yet the region they covered was fantastically great, stretching from St. Michael's Mission on Lake Pepin in Minnesota to Mobile, Alabama. As a parish priest serves two villages in our country today, Father Allouez, the Jesuit friend of Father Marquette, served two missions three hundred miles apart, one at Green Bay and one in Lower Illinois. The missionaries of the Mississippi were worthy peers of Father Marquette, but their harvest was pitiful.

And what patience the missionaries had need of ! Father Marest wrote from Kaskaskia a letter intended for ears which he was sure expected to hear fabulous stories of conversion. All he could say was : "Our life continues in the threading of thick forests, the dragging of one's self over the mountains, the crossing of lakes and rivers in a canoe, all to arrive at one poor savage who runs from us, and whom we cannot tame either by entreaty or by kindness." And when he wrote this letter he had been doing what he described and nothing else for fifteen years.

No — even aside from what scandals some French frontiersmen may have caused, and even aside from the hindrances set in their way by a French government growing more and more anti-clerical, even aside from the ecclesiastical quarrels that did exist between the different orders and between the secular and regular clergy, the missionaries were working at a most unrewarding task. The mission of the Immaculate Conception at Kaskaskia lasted for ninety years, ten times longer than the Jesuit missions among the Iroquois, yet where was a Catherine Tekakwitha ? Louisiana came to include some ten thousand French inhabitants, but it remained an Indian country. Yet how few hundred of those Indians were even ever baptized. When in 1763 the French flag in eastern Louisiana was hauled down, was it not a signal that another bubble had burst, the bubble of France's religious aspirations ? Could not the Jesuits and the others say : "We have worked for a century in vain. We have left nothing behind."

But I wonder. Was it not rather that their success was hidden as Our Lady's brilliance is always hidden ? Was not their work, which was so dedicated to her, wrought in her likeness ; did it not remain veiled, in the background ? Let us not look for proud positive statistics of baptisms. Let us look for what is humbler, and deeper.

It is not that we would stare into the void, where we can see what we wish to see by seeing what we imagine. It has always been remarked that the Indians for the most part fought as allies for the French against the English. And why ? I do not think that there is any dispute about the answer. It is not that the French were better at tricking them, nor that the French bribed them more handsomely with presents. It was that the French treated the Indians as human beings. It was not only the missionaries who did this. The French of all professions never had the fierce imperious racism of the so-called Anglo-Saxons. Soldiers, colonists and traders collaborated in this treatment. Take the attitude of such a man as Du Luth, after whom the present city of Duluth has been named. He was an adventurer, a trader, an ex-

plorer in Louisiana and New France at the end of the
seventeenth century.   Such a man had various reasons to
consider himself as being quite superior to the Indians.
He was not an ignorant bush-ranger, he was a man of
distinguished family, and of the superior French education that belonged to a man of his class.   He was moreover a successful man ; he had discovered the Falls of St.
Anthony in Minnesota the day after Father Hennepin
had discovered them.   He was an explorer and resourceful trader, and he ruled the Indians, though he held no
office, simply by the force of his personality.   He was a
power among the Indians, a power for justice and peace
almost anywhere that he happened to be.   And he well
knew the great superficial difference between an Indian
and a Frenchman.   Let Du Luth was on his knees to one
Indian : Catherine Tekakwitha.   She was in the next
world to be sure, but she was still an Indian.   Having
heard of her holy life and death — she was alive when he
was alive — he asked her intercession to cure him of his
gout.   And when his gout disappeared he publicly pro-
claimed his gratitude to her.

This sense of companionship with the Indians was
based on the Christian sense of an equality before God,
and it could not have existed without a sense among the
French of the supernatural.   It required a great confidence in God's mercy.   I doubt even if among Jan-
senists it might have existed.   It needed the humility, the
cheerfulness, the companionableness that Our Lady in-
culcates.   It could never have been created by the priests,
the missionaries alone, but neither could it have existed
without the priests.   It was not a merely natural thing

to be attributed to any racial affability of the French. It was the mark of France's Catholicism. It was the flowering of Our Lady's France, nurtured by Our Lady's priests.

But the French priests had another effect which they, and they alone, were responsible for. They impressed on the Indians, on the Indians of our entire Northwest, the idea of the Christian priesthood. They did it not by methods of catechism, but by the patient, seemingly futile, method of example. They created their own legend, made the picture of the Black Robe (a name used originally only of Jesuit priests, but later of all priests) that stayed in the imagination of the Indians of the northern half of the United States. In Maine, in Upper New York State, and throughout all the Mississippi Valley to the Rocky Mountains, the Black Robe became the man of prestige, the White Man who was the White Man of White Men. He was brave as a warrior, yet he did not kill. He went farther than the fur-trader, but he sought no profit. In their Indian traditions there was a place for asceticism; he was an ascetic. In their traditions there was a place for men who were set apart as if in special favor and communication with this or that god. These priests were men who were being used by the Author of Life. The Indians did not wish to change incautiously their customs, and to adopt the moral law of Christians. But into their traditions they accepted the Black Robe.

After 1763 when France had left Louisiana, an Englishman decided to go down the Mississippi from Canada, by the road which the French had used so freely in their community with the Indians. It would be death, he was told. Death — unless he dressed like a Black Robe ; then he might pass.

In the nineteenth century, when our nation was still young, Catholic priests began to penetrate again into the French regions west of the Mississippi. There was hazard to the penetration unless there was strong escort, for the Indians were generally on the warpath against the intruders. But even without escort a Catholic priest was safe. The Indians would gallop up and circle him while his heart beat its terror-strokes. Then they would hail him as a Black Robe, the Black Robe of the Indian legends, even of Indian pagan legends. And he would thank God for the marvel of it, sometimes trying to puzzle out why it should be.

Once there was an even greater marvel, a marvel which, like the key to a code, enables us to read the true meaning of all of France's missionary effort in our midst. It came to pass that the legend of the Black Robes penetrated in the first decade of the nineteenth century to an obscure valley of the Rocky Mountains, to the Flat Head Indians of Montana. And who had brought the legend there ? Who but the Iroquois originally of New York State, who had so long been the chief enemies of the Black Robes, who had been the martyr-makers of our continent, and whom the Black Robes had bought with their best blood ? These Iroquois, a band of them, had immigrated to the Flat Head country, and there had stayed. They had told the Flat Heads of the Black Robes. These Flat Heads from hearing of the Black Robes wished that they might have such men among

them, for they worshipped a Creator, and the Black
Robes, they decided, must be special agents of the
Creator.

News came to them — we wonder how — that Black
Robes had arrived in the old French settlement of St.
Louis.   This was in 1830, and there was no telegraph and
no mail, and the Oregon Trail had not begun, and St.
Louis was a thousand miles away.   Undaunted by dis-
tance and by the hostile Sioux tribes between them and
St. Louis, they held a council and appointed four of their
number to go to bring back to them a Black Robe.

The four arrived at St. Louis.   But once arrived there,
no one could understand their tongue.   Two of them
died of the plague, and died kissing the crucifix that a
priest held to their lips.   The other two who had somehow received a promise that a Black Robe would be sent
to them died on their return journey, slain by the Sioux.

Those in Montana who waited their return — waited
and waited.   One day some White Men arrived, ready
to preach to them, and to preach Christ, but they had
wives, and they had no Mass, and the Flat Heads who
knew no theology did not recognize them as Black Robes.
They were Methodists who had heard of the strange visit
to St. Louis and who genuinely thought that they possessed what the Flat Heads wanted.   The Flat Heads
made no comment, but refused to listen.   The Methodists moved on.

The next time it was an aged Iroquois who made the
journey.   It was he who had told the Flat Heads of the
Black Robes, and he was a Christian.   He knew the
French language ; he would go.   He went with his two

sons. This was in 1835. He saw the Bishop of St. Louis, Rosati, confessed his sins, saw to it that his sons were baptized, received again a promise of a Black Robe. Returned. But no Black Robe. Two years later he made the journey again. This time he was slain on his return journey.

Finally a fourth embassy set out in 1840. This time the Black Robes had a priest to spare. Father De Smet, of whom we shall hear more later, went to the Rockies. "Our meeting," he said speaking of his arrival at the Flat Heads', "was not that of strangers but of friends." Friends indeed ! But the friendship had been made by the French. That part of France's work that had been most true to France's consecration to Our Lady had a touch of eternity to it.

CHAPTER VI

MARYLAND

THEY HAVE their exits and their entrances — was said of men, but it is just as true of nations. First Spain held the stage in our country, then France, now it was England. England had been blundering in the wings, and she came on the stage almost without meaning to, but the stage was certainly hers. She had all Spain's lands east of the Mississippi — that is she had the Florida of Menéndez — and she had the French lands east of the Mississippi. And she had a strength, like that of a suddenly grown boy who has a strength and does not know it. While she was not looking, her strange squatter colonies had grown powerful and populous. They could act for her, and who could act against her? And what then was to be her project? What would she do on the stage?

England does not really concoct projects, except purely down-to-the-ground commercial ones. She does things, and then lets the historians decide what they were, and her pragmatic moralists decide how they were justified. If a cautious prophet had been asked, however, what he thought England would do in this new territory, he would have made with every sense of security one cautious — laughably cautious — prophecy: England will put an end to any relation that Our Lady has or has had with these lands. But let not even the cautious be prophets. Thirty years later Our Lady had appeared and reappeared resplendent in this domain that had fallen to England's lot.   She was not the acknowledged sovereign, the "conquistadora," as she had been among the Spaniards and French.   But she had made her entry with the English as she had made her entry with the Spanish and French.   It seemed as if she met each nation on the threshold of our country, and in her manner, infinite in variety, worked with them.

When the first English came to our shores, sailing under the Italian Cabots, England was in her own conception Our Lady's special realm, Our Lady's Dower. Whether other parts of Christendom would have been willing to concede her that preeminence I very much doubt, for as every people now in the world considers that it is honest and sincere in comparison with its perfidious neighbors, so every part of old Christendom assumed as a matter of course that it was most especially Our Lady's.   Yet England had still at that time some title to be called Our Lady's Dower.   When an Englishman in 1500 made his written testament he began it true to English custom : "First, I bequeathe my soul to God Almighty and to our holy lady Saint Mary, and to all the fair company of hevene."   When a group of Englishmen happened to form a corporation or guild at that late date, it would begin its charter after this manner : "In the worshippe of our lord and of our levedy Sainte Marie."   England, at the time of Columbus, had still her shrine of Our Lady at Walsingham, which was so important that Erasmus — who hated vulgar pilgrimages — had to make a pilgrimage to it, and did there write a Greek poem in Our Lady's honor.   And England's niggard King, Henry VII, who sent the first English ships to the New World, was himself bountiful to that shrine. And so confidently did Englishmen think of the road to that shrine as a permanent road, that the Milky Way, the starry road in the sky, also never changing, they called Walsingham Way. England of old had been an innovator in rites that celebrated Our Lady's Immaculate Conception. Then England had her Duns Scotus in order to define that Immaculate Conception. And though Duns Scotus had passed, Our Lady stayed.

But before the English had come to our shores really to settle those shores, all this had changed. Walsingham had been destroyed.

"Weep, weep, O Walsingham," sang the popular song.

> "Weep, weep, O Walsingham
> Whose days are nights :
> Blessings turned to blasphemies,
> Holy deeds to despites ;
> Sin is where Our Lady sate
> Heaven turned is to Hell ;
> Satan sits where Our Lady did sway —
> Walsingham, O, farewell."

No longer did England touch the sky where Our Lady ruled. Her sky was her earthly sovereign's sky, King Henry VIII's, Queen Elizabeth's.

Yet, curiously enough, this change seemed destined to make the English colonies on the other side of the Atlantic Our Lady's Dower, by transporting there those who wished still to belong to Our Lady. When England took to herself a nationalistic religion, and a national church, she left out of its tidy happiness two groups of people, two discontented classes, two species of non-conformists, one of which wished that the old religion, untrimmed, were back, the other that every trace of it were abolished. The first were much the more numerous. They were the Catholics ; the second were fewer and much more aggressive — they were the Calvinists. These more numerous non-conformists, who were — it goes without saying — those who wished that England were still Our Lady's Dower, had particularly no place in England. Yet they were pertinaciously English. It occurred, therefore, to some of England's statesmen that one way to let them stay English, yet have them out of the country, was to send them across the water as colonists. Let them be transatlantic Englishmen. They were the obvious colonists. Let them build far away, where it would do no harm, Our Lady's Dower.

Sir Humphrey Gilbert, Protestant, planned to use them this way, and the Queen — Queen Elizabeth — fell in with his plan. In 1582 he filled a ship called, indirectly, after Our Lady, the *Delight*, with a hundred of these outlaw Catholics. It sailed toward the State of Maine, but sank off the coast of Nova Scotia, and Sir Humphrey Gilbert sank too.

Then some Catholic nobles began to make this scheme which had originally been a Protestant scheme their Catholic scheme. The Earl of Arundel, Henry Wardour, a Catholic, planned a settlement of Catholics also in Maine. This time the ship did not sink. It arrived in Maine. A cross was set up, a bay was called Pentecost Bay, but the ship sailed back to England — we know not why. And this was in 1604, still three years before the real settling of Jamestown.

Yet it was not the Catholics who became the great English colonizers of America; it was the other nonconformists, the Calvinists. The Catholics liked England too well to leave it. They had put their roots of affection into the soil as Catholics always do; and they stayed at home, hoping for better days. Also they had no patrons with money enough to send them across the water. On the other hand, Calvinists tend to be unsocial to their environment and to their neighbors; thus they were readier to immigrate. And there were rich English capitalists who were shrewd enough to see what admirable and useful transatlantic Englishmen they would make. To begin with they were thrifty, good for trade. Then by their religion they hated Spain, and, though not corsairs, would not interfere with the corsair activity of the English merchants if it were against the Spaniards. And these moneyed merchants, though not religious, did not like Catholics, for the name Catholic reminded them of the source of their wealth — loot from the church — which was something that they tried to forget. They preferred to be with Calvinists, even though they had an antipathy for fanaticism.

It is well to take a look at one of these English speculators close to in order to appreciate how it came about that such men chose the Calvinists as partners, and could continue with them. And which of them is better to look at than one, the most conspicuous of them all, the Earl of Warwick?

I have an idea that the Earl of Warwick was, to walk

with and dine with, and fight on the same side with, a charming man. He had none of the self-righteousness of the worst of the Calvinists, none of the lack of urbanity of the best of them. He was a sociable being. He was travelled, well read, witty, courageous in battle, as adventurous as a naughty schoolboy, carefree, ready to be friendly and hospitable in his pleasures, not intellectually proud, nor spiritually, and not argumentative. And though he was an unscrupulous money-getter, money-getting was a game with him ; he was not avaricious. And though he played the hypocrite, he did it lightly, merely allowing others to be fooled by him, if they were fool enough. There was adventure in him.

At the same time, the history of the man stands, and it is not lovable. To begin with — though we blame it not on him — his grandfather was the notorious Richard Rich who perjured himself at the trial of Saint Thomas More in order to win royal favor, and who gained excessive reward by securing the ex-chancellor's conviction. Richard Rich became Sir Richard Rich and had a son who kept his father's ill-gotten wealth, and added to it, without adding to his ignominy. Then came the Rich which I refer to as the Earl of Warwick. He was in reality the second of that title. He was Robert Rich, the second Robert Rich.

The second earl dared take risks that his forbears avoided. He was an enterprising developer of England's foreign trade, and when that foreign trade took the form of piracy, so much the better ; there was more of a lark in it. He was one of those who sent the English colony to Jamestown. He lost money on Jamestown but I suspect he expected to. Jamestown was worth losing money on. It was a place from which the Caribbean could be raided, and through the possession of which any such losses could be made up ; for Jamestown, as the early governor said, needed for its prosperity but two things — a good tobacco crop and "a fair war" with Spain. Even when there was no fair war, an unfair war could be arranged. The Earl of Warwick turned pirate, but not openly. He sailed under the flag of the Duke of Savoy, who was then at war with Spain, and did his piracy with proper respectability.

In founding Jamestown, the Earl of Warwick and his companions had not utilized the Puritans. They were not exactly his kind, and he had not discovered his affinity with them. But the colonists which he had to use, being vaguely irreligious, were not of a usefulness that recommended them to him. They were generally good-for-nothings, lazy, vicious, giving no strength to the settlement. After that experiment he preferred to use Puritans. They were earnest, obstinate, law-abiding. He became therefore the great promoter of the Calvinistic colonies, of Plymouth, of Boston, of Rhode Island (though the last was not exactly Calvinistic) — and of Connecticut. It was his particular grant of land which was, so it is now thought, the grant that was given to the Massachusetts Bay Colony. He became, though continuing to be a black-leg and epicurean, an ally of the Puritans. He became what Clarendon called the "Temporal Head of the Puritans," and very temporal at that. He played Puritanism for profit, and was, so also said Clarendon, the only Englishman who made money out of the War of the Revolution against King Charles.

Associated with the Earl of Warwick were other financial promoters, some of them more unscrupulous some less, but all of them less daring than he. These men wedded the Calvinists with the gold ring of money, and the marriage lasted. Together they formed a Protestant, or anti-Catholic, front, which gave a strength to the English colonies, for the merchants supplied the shrewdness and the Puritans the fanaticism. Although not the only element on the English Atlantic seaboard, the two working together gave the spiritual tone to all the colonies. Together they drew over the Anglican colonists into non-conformism, and created that anti-prelatic spirit on this side of the ocean which frightened the Church of England from ever daring to send a bishop into the colonies, even though in various of those colonies the Church of England was by law the established Church.

Thus instead of becoming Our Lady's Dower, Transatlantic England became quite the opposite. It would be an insult to it to say that it was a fortress against her, for even the Calvinists in their beliefs had a place to honor her, but she was not its sovereign. And she was not the joy of the land. The Calvinists did not wish to derive any joy from her or from any other human being. They resented joy. What Henry Adams said of them is somewhat true! "The Puritans abandoned the New Testament and the Virgin in order to go back to the beginning and renew the quarrel with Eve." The Puritans certainly rejected the traditional joyfulness of Christendom, and the cause of it also. And their spirit dominated in all the colonies.

Yet strangely enough into this anti-Marial stronghold was inserted a Marial colony. It was not one of the old English Catholic nobles who had established it, but one of these new men of energy, the class that was making imperial England, the moneyed men. He was George Calvert, one of the most enterprising of the class to which he belonged, a wise promoter of foreign trade, an active shareholder in many a commercial venture. But he was more than that : he was a man of probity, and a man wise in the affairs of state, the principal secretary of state to Charles I. He was able to found such a colony because he was an able man of affairs, but also because he had the King's respect. And the reason he wanted to found it was that, unlike many of the merchants, he gave ultimate things some thought, and having decided that truth and salvation lay in the Catholic Church, he determined to enter it, cost what it might. And then he determined to help his fellow-Catholics.

It did cost him something to become a Catholic ; he had to cease to hold public office, but Charles I was truer to him than to some of his friends, and simply for friendship gave him the title Lord Baltimore, protected him from penal laws, left him in his very great wealth, and allowed him, in an act of confidence hard to explain, to establish a colony north of Virginia in the New World over which he could be feudal lord with the rarest privileges of autonomy such as belonged in England only to the County Palatine of Durham. His obligations to the King were to be a payment of a share of the precious metals, if such were there to be found, but otherwise only a nominal payment of arrow-heads — symbolic as an act of fealty. — This colony was not to be a specifically Catholic refuge, but it was to be a refuge to which Catholics could escape from persecution as well as others of any other persecuted sect, for the religion of the colony was written down merely as the "true Christian Religion" without any definition as to what that religion was. In other words it was to be a place where people could live together, provided they wanted to live a Christian life, even though they differed in their conception of it, and even though they differed in their conception of it zealously.

It has been suggested that the conception of such a colony, tolerating all but fanaticism, was derived from the Utopia of Saint Thomas More. That the head of the English Jesuits at this time was Father Henry More, descendant of Saint Thomas, and that it was the Jesuits who accompanied the colonizing expedition when it took place, lends color to this suggestion. And if it is so, then the colony of Lord Baltimore derives from Saint Thomas More, whereas the other English colonies derive from Sir Richard Rich, who betrayed him — which is hard — all too hard on the other colonies. But mayhap the idea of toleration came from Lord Baltimore's practical sense, from his knowledge of affairs, and from his experience with human beings. At any rate, the idea became his. And he being a man who accomplished things, the colony came into being. In 1634 the *Ark* and the *Dove* arrived in the bay which the Spaniards a hundred years before had christened the Bay

of the Mother of God — Chesapeake Bay. They were
the ships of Lord Baltimore, though he was dead. With
them was one of his sons, Leonard. His other son, Cecil,
who had married the daughter of the Earl of Arundel and
thus connected the project with the earlier Catholic
colonizing projects, remained in England with the office
of governor. On the Feast of the Annunciation, March
25, the colonists landed on St. Clement's Island in the
Potomac River, and there the two Jesuit priests celebrated the colony's first Mass. It was an act which belonged specifically not to the whole colony, but to the
Catholics of it, who were the influential minority. Yet
it was astounding on the anti-Catholic seaboard of the
English New World to have such an act take place without
interference or heckling or grimaces of discontent. Such
did not occur. Then the colony was given a name. It
was Maryland. The name in the minds of the Catholics
recalled Our Lady, but officially it was but a compliment
to Henrietta Maria, Queen of England. Thus Our Lady
did enter into the English colonies, but not ostentatiously
— "as still as dew that falleth on the grass."

This colony, with its feudal origin, was, curiously
enough, the most democratic of all the English colonies
in America, for the Proprietor allowed it to make its
own laws like a New England town meeting, and unlike the early New England town meetings, there was
no restricted franchise. Every man had his vote, irre-
spective of wealth, or church membership. As a check
on any wildness of omnipotent legislation, there was first
the governor's veto, and second the unwritten precept
of the first Lord Baltimore that theological bickering

was to be prohibited.   This later precept became a part of the common law of Maryland.   Within the first decade of Maryland's founding, the courts of Maryland had established it.   There was in Maryland a Catholic named Lewis who happened to overhear a Protestant hour of worship echoing through an open window.   It was not a Protestant minister's voice, for there was no Protestant minister in the colony, but the Protestant laymen were reading aloud some minister's quite impassioned sermon. Lewis, listening to the reading, heard the Pope and the Jesuits being reviled and reviled again, and losing his temper he shouted out that the author of such stuff was an instrument of the Devil.   For this offense he was tried and by Catholic judges was convicted and forced to pay a fine of 500 pounds of tobacco.   It was not a question of the truth or falsity of his words : he had "disturbed the peace by unreasonable disputation."   The Catholics of Maryland acted with extraordinary discretion.   They were not half-hearted in their faith.   They called manfully and openly Maryland's first little capital city St. Mary's, but they made no attempt to give Catholics special privileges.   The priests of the colony received no public funds, no public recognition.   They supported themselves as private owners of farms.   Their chapels even were private, and were on private property though the Catholics used them as parish churches.

So discreet and neighborly were the Catholics of Maryland that it would have seemed that they were due to receive the neighborliness of all.   And such was the case with the Protestants who had to associate with them in Maryland.   But with outsiders it was different.   During the Civil Wars in England, between King and Parliament, Governor Berkeley of Virginia who sided with the King drove some Puritans who were of the Parliament Party out of Virginia. Maryland in trustfulness offered them an asylum in her territory. There they were, in any ordinary sense, not ill treated, but they considered that a positive outrage was done them in making them take an oath "not to insult any other man's religion, not even the Roman Catholic one." They rose in rebellion, and soon the Marylanders, Protestant and Catholic, were ranged in battle against these difficult guests. According to the Puritan account the war cry of the Marylanders was: "Hey for Saint Marie." Their answer was: "In the name of God fall on: God is our strength." The Puritans won the battle. The Marylanders, St. Mary's party, surrendered on promise of quarter, and found immediately that ten of their number were condemned to death, of whom four were executed. It seemed as if Our Lady's colony was to cease to be Our Lady's.

But a curious thing happened. Oliver Cromwell — of all people — bade the Puritans to put an end to their quarrelsomeness. He restored the colony to Lord Baltimore. Something of the original spirit of the colony continued.

The next menace came from another source. In 1689, King William III came to the throne of England, whereupon a Marylander called Coode complained to him that Maryland, infested with Catholics, had stood out against him in favor of James II whom he had dethroned. Coode had been once a Catholic, then had pretended to be a Protestant, but according to the Protestants his pretense was not good ; he was an atheist.   One thing sure, he was a troublemaker, and a clever one.   Whether William III was deceived by him, or pretended to be deceived by him we do not know, but at any rate he saw to it that the charter of Maryland was abrogated.   The province was taken from the Calverts, and it reverted to the Crown.   In so doing it lost its privileges which the first Calvert had secured for it.   Automatically the English National Church became established there, and all the inhabitants had to support it, except the Puritans and the Protestant non-conformists, who were exempted therefrom by special decree of the King.   Legally now the Catholics were, as they were in England, outlaws. They could have no civil rights, they could not practise the liberal professions, they could not attend Mass. Priests were forbidden them.   If a Catholic taught school he was liable to a year's imprisonment.   The Catholic who employed a Catholic teacher, even as a private tutor, had to pay thirty shillings for every day he had so employed him.   If a Catholic sent his son to Europe the fine was 100 pounds.

All this was true legally.   In reality there were enough Protestant Marylanders who liked the old ways of Maryland too well to let the laws be applied.   They knew there were Jesuits still in Maryland — everyone knew it — but they chose not to notice them, or not to notice that they were Jesuits : they were neighbors that had long been there.   Of course, the Catholics who were poor and unknown, who were indentured servants, who were newcomers, suffered great spiritual privations.   They could not go, as the rich did, to Europe for the Sacrament of Confirmation. They could not possibly give their children anything but a Protestant education. They could enjoy no social parish life. Such did not exist. But for the old Maryland Catholic families, and for the rich and well-thought-of, life was tolerable. The Carrolls, the richest of the Catholic families, did not hesitate to send their children to a Jesuit primary school, and they were not fined. And they sent their sons regularly to St. Omer's in France to complete their education without giving a second thought to the penalty of 100 pounds.

Yet how long would this condition of affairs continue? In 1754 a double tax was levied on Catholics, even on the Carrolls, and the Carrolls grew restive. In 1760 while the war with France was going on, in the excitement of the moment, it was proposed in the Maryland Assembly to confiscate the lands of all Catholics. France was Catholic, therefore the Maryland Catholics were their allies. Such reasoning was nonsense, and the best Marylanders knew it, but the Catholics could not help seeing that they were dependent on the good-will of a political body over which they had no influence, into which they could not enter, and which like any other such body could in times of weakness try to feel strong with fanaticism.

Contrary to what might have been expected and hoped by Catholics, the victory of England over France in the Seven Years' War, and the Peace of 1763, did not bring a lull in the rising tide of anti-Catholic feeling in Maryland, nor in the pressure exerted by other provinces on Maryland that she join their utterly intolerant rank, that she conform to the anti-Catholic conformity. Three hundred Catholic Marylanders, seeing the lowering sky, moved off into Kentucky where on a frontier their Catholicism would not be watched. He who was then chief of the Carrolls, the father of Charles Carroll of Carrollton, negotiated with the King of Spain for the purchase of lands in Spanish Louisiana. He was ready in a sad readiness to move there, and was dissuaded from the move only by the tardiness of Spain's King and by the expostulations of his son.

In 1774 there came a climax to this anti-Catholic madness. It was England's Parliament that brought the climax by passing in that year the Quebec Act, which countenanced the toleration of Catholics and of Catholic priests both in Canada and in the region west of the Alleghanies. This move was dictated both by justice and by expediency. By the treaty of peace, eleven years before, England had bound herself to respect the religion of the French citizens in the New World whom she had taken over, and those regions were inhabited by French citizens who were Catholics. And how could she ever make them happy and contented under the English flag without some act of friendliness? And she needed to have them friendly, and with them the Indians. Nevertheless, the act was interpreted in the English colonies as a surrender to the Babylon of Catholic Rome, and the roar which arose along the Atlantic seaboard was like the breaking of a tidal wave which had for generations been rolling from a distant horizon. Ezra Stiles, President of Yale College, cried out that it established "Romish Religion and Idolatry" over two-thirds of English Amer-

ica.   Samuel Adams demanded — merely I believe for the
sake of oratory — that an investigation of Massachusetts
towns be made to discover whether or not they were infested with "Popery" — and this at a time when fifty or
sixty Catholics, cringing and helpless, were all that were
in the province.   A Philadelphian was equally alarmed!
"We may live to see our churches converted into mass-
houses and our lands plundered of tythes for the support
of a Popish clergy.   The Inquisition may erect her
standard in Pennsylvania, and the city of Philadelphia
may yet experience the carnage of St. Bartholomew's
Day."   All this sounds like hysteria, but in soberer terms
the same consternation was expressed by the Continental
Congress meeting then in Philadelphia.   It addressed the
people of Great Britain: "We think the Legislature of
Great Britain is not authorized by the Constitution to
establish a religion, fraught with sanguinary and impious
tenets — ."

Sanguinary tenets!   The Catholic Marylanders were
holders of these sanguinary tenets.   Their doom was
sealed.   The ship was sinking under the Marylanders.
And yet the next instant the ship was safe.   The colonies
suddenly took up arms against their mother country,
and it was as if the wind had changed, as if the change
of wind had blown the sea smooth.   And the Marylanders found the sky smiling on them.   Their neighbors
were saying to themselves, "We need Catholic help."

Washington needed the military help of the Catholic
nations, France and Spain.   Let the Continental troops
at Boston give up their practice of burning the effigy of
the Pope on Guy Fawkes' Day.   Let the Abenakis of

Maine be allowed a Catholic chaplain which they ask for in order that they may march to Cambridge.

And the Continental Congress realized the need they had for Maryland's aid. Maryland was in population far more Protestant than Catholic, yet Maryland's richest man and chief citizen was a Catholic — Charles Carroll of Carrollton. He was more than that : he was the richest man in all the colonies, and though not so forceful a personality as John Adams, or the great men of Virginia, he was probably the most urbane man in North America, for he had received an education in France, and also in England, having in that latter country studied law even though he knew that, as a Catholic, he could not practise it. Charles Carroll was in control of valuable iron works. He was also in control of Maryland's public opinion. He was already disposed, even eager, to join the colonists against England. In no way must he be offended. And he was not. He was in every way honored.

And then there was the question of Canada. Should Canada join whole-heartedly against them, then their northern frontier was in dire danger. Canada was composed of French Catholics who were not such fools as not to remember the Protestant fanaticism of the English colonists. So the most persuasive embassy possible was sent northward. It was composed of Samuel Chase of Maryland, an urbane man, not fanatic, and of Benjamin Franklin, even more urbane, and of Charles Carroll of Carrollton, who was a Catholic. And finally to give the embassy a clerical look, there was added to it as secretary, a priest whom John Adams commended for his learning and personally chose : John Carroll, a cousin of Charles. The embassy failed, but it had its significance as a gesture.

This change of front might well have been laughed at by some. Benedict Arnold after he had turned traitor raged at it. It happened that shortly before his treason the members of the Continental Congress — a fairly large number of them — had attended a Requiem Mass for the repose of the soul of Miralles, the envoy of the King of Spain to Washington's army, at St. Joseph's Church in Philadelphia. The attendance of course was an act of diplomatic courtesy, but even then it had little precedent. Arnold in order to justify his own betrayal of the colonies pointed to this betrayal by the members of the Congress of their Protestant allegiance. "Do you know that the eye that guides this pen," he wrote in 1780, "lately saw your mean and profligate Congress at Mass for the soul of a Roman Catholic in purgatory?"

Yet this change of face was more significant than merely to be laughed at. It was not mere opportunism. There was a spiritual awakening behind it. The sudden war with its new circumstances and problems waked the colonial leaders out of an outgrown provincialism, and also presented the colonists with new leaders. These men were not playing the hypocrite. They could not help seeing that "Down with the Pope" could not serve as their battle cry against Protestant England, and they began to suspect that it was not their battle cry at all. Liberty had become their battle cry. They did not recognize their cry as a Catholic one. They were quite unaware that liberty with a large L was but a cutting from a plant in Catholic theology. They considered it as something from ancient Greece or Rome. Yet in the name of Liberty how could they treat Catholics as helots?

The coming of the war saved the Marylanders from a persecution that might have annihilated them. The winning of the war had a further consequence; it made the Marylanders conspicuous, because of their tradition — never quite obliterated — of toleration. The builders of the new nation were quite aware that one of the great difficulties in regard to establishing concord and peace among the thirteen colonies was the fact that there were deep and genuine religious differences among those who inhabited those States. This was a day before religious indifferentism had set in. Two-thirds of the books in English North America were, the historians tell us, religious books, which can legitimately be classed as religious even though at least a half of them were only negatively so, being attacks on the Catholic Church. Theology was taken very seriously. Maryland was the only colony where there was a long tradition of men keeping the peace even though they disagreed vehemently on matters of faith. She could not help being looked at.

At first those who looked at Maryland and looked at themselves decided that the matter must not be made a national matter at all. Every State except Pennsylvania had its established Church. Let each State continue to have the established church it wanted. As the Federal constitution was first adopted it did not mention religion at all. But there was always a possibility that in some future time the National Government might become affiliated with some one of the sects. Some such sect might become the Federal Church. Although each sect would have been satisfied with such a solution provided that it was the sect that was so honored, mutual jealousy led them to prevent forever any such victory for any one of them. So the Maryland solution of the problem — Lord Baltimore's solution — was incorporated verbally into the constitution. It was not the Catholics who insisted on this. Of what importance were they alone? It was the Protestants. Yet it is significant that Maryland citizens were especially called upon to phrase Maryland's custom into our first amendment. Charles Carroll of Carrollton, now a Senator, was chairman of the committee appointed to draught the amendment. His cousin Daniel Carroll made in his favor the most important speech in the House of Representatives. The amendment was phrased : "Congress shall make no laws respecting an establishment of religion, or prohibiting free exercise thereof." It was passed. It entered our Constitution on the same wind that brought over the *Ark* and the *Dove*.

Maryland's way had become the way of the Federal Government. Such was the extraordinary turn-over that took place when our new nation saw itself not merely as a string of colonies dependent on England and threatened by France and Spain, but as a nation among nations ; when it came to act as if it were of age, on a scene that was the world. And all this change had come about in fifteen years.

This marvel was matched by another marvel. In the very year in which George Washington became the first President, John Carroll, the priest whom John Adams had found to be a "gentleman of learning and abilities" and whom he had sent as secretary on the diplomatic mission to Montreal, and whom Franklin on that mission had found to be a most kindly and considerate nurse — for Franklin at the age of seventy was camping out on his way to Canada like a school-boy and needed a nurse — was appointed Bishop of Baltimore, with the United States as his diocese.

The land which had so detested the name of bishop that even the English King had dared not send an Anglican bishop to its shores, had been by the curious train of events drawn to approve of such an appointment and invite it. Our young nation in its new pride was obsessed with the word independence. If she were to have Catholics in her midst they must have the privileges of other Catholics. They should have their own bishop, or even more important, they should not have to look to an English bishop, who living in England would have a shadow of English control over our land. Mr. John Carroll, as he was called, was not only a resident bishop, a new dignity to our country, but he was an American of Americans ; his family name stood for American Independence. His cousin Charles had signed it to the Declaration. His cousin Daniel had presented a large part of the land for the future city of Washington where the seat of that Independence should be established. It is true that the news of his appointment as bishop did not make a great noise everywhere in the colonies. Catholics were but one in every hundred of the population, and their general importance was much less than that proportion would indicate. They were not even thought about. There were no thoughts in which they could be thought about. They were like books which cannot be catalogued. But those who knew of it, men like John Adams, President Washington, Benjamin Franklin (who was on his death-bed when the news came), were gratified. It was like a ratification of the permanent independence of their land.

Bishop-elect was the title which Mr. Carroll had gained in 1789. The next year he was consecrated. In order to find bishops to consecrate him he had to leave the United States, no bishop of any kind having ever set foot on what was then the United States, — Florida and New Mexico being still Spain's. — He went to Europe and was consecrated in England in the chapel of Lulworth Castle by an aged Benedictine, Bishop Walmesley. The chapel was one dedicated to Our Lady, and the day was the feast of her Assumption. "Mr. Carroll," as soon as he became Bishop Carroll, adopted a seal for his diocese on which was pictured Our Lady surrounded by stars. Under her were St. Peter's keys.

One of the first people to congratulate him after his consecration was an Earl of Arundel, descendant of the Earl of Arundel who had planned to make the New England in the New World into the Catholic England which Old England had for the time ceased to be. Nothing like what he had planned had ever come to pass. The English across the water had not become a Catholic New England — most certainly not. Yet the Earl had something on which to thank and congratulate the new bishop, for the bishop stood for the fruition of at least some of the prayers and efforts of the Earl's ancestors. It was the remnant of Catholic England that had created Maryland. And because of Maryland, Our Lady had been able, through the English as through the French and the Spanish, to go her sovereign way. She had, through the handful of English who named their colony somewhat hiddenly after her, presented her particular charge and treasure, the Catholic priesthood, to a new nation which did not know what it was.

CHAPTER VII

BISHOP JOHN CARROLL

SALVE REGINA." One of the first things that Bishop Carroll did when he returned to his diocese, the United States, was to order that regularly before the celebration of High Mass, the Litany of Loretto — or the Litany of Our Lady — should be recited.

And good need he had of litanies and Our Lady's help, for he was faced with a task in which to fail would mean catastrophe, in which to succeed he would need more ability than he or any man could have. He had been presented with a diocese three million square miles in extent, and had been told to watch over and direct the Catholics within it. He could not himself visit all that immense area, nor could he find priests to do it for him. Those who were trustworthy were busy where they were. Those who were free were untrustworthy. And how could he pay their travelling expenses? And how could he wait for their return? And after they returned how could he act on what they reported? His diocese was much more huge, much more unknowable than all our country is today. There were no facilities for inter-colonial tourists; there were none for commercial travelers. The Atlantic Ocean would have seemed to our eyes to have offered a fair road between the ten colonies that lived on it, but even up to 1800 it was easier to arrange for a passage from New York to London than

from New York to Boston.   There was one land road
from Portland, Maine, to Savannah, Georgia, with stage-
coaches on it that started off three times a week, but the
coaches moved at four miles an hour, and at the expensive rate of six cents to the mile.   It took three weeks to
go the length of the seacoast.   As for going inland —
to Tennessee, for example, which was part of the bishop's
diocese — roads need not be thought of except the roads
that nature had made and that General Braddock had
added to when attacking the French.   A westward voy-
ager could go up the Potomac, cross the Alleghanies,
descend by the Ohio to Tennessee.   He could do it in
three weeks.   But so arduous and expensive was the return trip that it was best to take as many months to make
it by descending the Mississippi and returning to Baltimore by sea.   Bishop Carroll was a man of frail health,
and he was already nearly sixty, and he was not made
for the wilderness.   He never visited the land beyond
the mountains.   To have visited it and left the affairs
of Baltimore behind him would, during certain periods
of his office, have been tantamount to an abdication.

But it was not only the size of his diocese that made
his task impossible.   It was also the nature and appor-
tionment of its Catholic population.   There were thirty-
six thousand Catholics estimated as being his in 1790.
Nearly thirty thousand of them were near him in Maryland.   They were the least of his problems, though owing to persecution and to the scarcity of priests there
were but little over half of them that received Holy Communion as often as once a year.   They were not all ex-
emplary, nor were they all like brothers in one house,

for some were English-speaking, some German, and they did not always know how to surmount their national prejudices.   Also they had never been used to support-ing a clergy.   The clergy under the old Calvert plan had supported themselves from their own lands.

But the Marylanders were the least of the problem.   It was the six thousand others that would have kept a bishop sleepless.   They were first the Germans of Pennsylvania, who were difficult to rule over, but who nevertheless were concentrated in a single district where they could be dealt with.   There were secondly the French, say two thousand of them, in the region west of the mountains, in old Upper Louisiana.   And finally there were the scat-tered Catholics, everywhere, nowhere.

The difficulty in regard to the French was mainly that the English had not yet evacuated Detroit and the other forts in their midst.   Their lands had not yet, except on paper, become a part of the United States.   And it was not well for Bishop Carroll to enter too authoritatively into that region as if his jurisdiction were assured.   But most of all beyond his control were the scattered Cath-olics, the hundred in Massachusetts, the hundred in South Carolina, the half a dozen in North Carolina, the two or three hundreds in New York, the thousand in all, numeri-cally unimportant, who were to be important as the foun-dation of the Church in the districts where formerly no Catholics had been allowed, and where now some degree of toleration had been introduced.   These Catholics were undiscernible, for they had been used so long to hide that they still hid.   Even when found they were often not reliable.   If they were rich they were cocky and wished

to have priests do what they commanded.   Most of them
were poor, and not a few of them had deliberately chosen
poverty, for they had clung to their faith when so to do
was to cut off their opportunities for advancement.
They had stayed with their faith when they had seen
their relatives who turned renegade grow prosperous and
turn against them even as persecutors.   They were Irish,
they were French.   Some of these heroic people were
very holy, but they had grown used to shifting for themselves ; and though they were such as a bishop's heart
went out to most, they were unprepared to receive it.
Merely that a man was a bishop meant little to them, that
he was a Carroll meant nothing unless they came from
around Maryland.

When Rome had decided to create a bishopric in the
United States, she had asked the priests there to vote for
one of their number as the most appropriate to occupy
the see.   Twenty-five had voted, and twenty-four — we
can imagine who the exception was — had voted for Mr.
John Carroll, then the Prefect Apostolic.   There were
thus surely twenty-four priests besides Bishop Carroll in
the United States when he began his work.   There were
also just as surely eleven others, who might have wished
to vote for him, but who could not attend the voting :
they were known of.   Besides that, there were undoubt-
edly other priests, unknown at Baltimore, and some of
them wishing to be unknown, laboring or hiding in our
country.   Bishop Carroll had then a corps of thirty-six
helpers.   But would they help ?   Almost half of them
could not help him very long, for they were old.   They
were the Maryland Jesuits who had been ordained before

the suppression of the Jesuits in 1773. They knew Maryland. They knew the spirit behind our struggle for independence for they had lived through it. But they were rather too old to be able to be of use in the States whose ways were not like Maryland's — Massachusetts' for instance. And they could not live forever. And also as members of an order that had been suppressed they were considered by some as entitled to be received with suspicion.

The rest of the priests were very clearly differentiated from the old ones. It was not that they were merely younger. They belonged to a generation which had scarcely touched the older generation. There was a gap between them. They knew nothing of old Maryland. They had not lived in America during the War of Independence. They had come over after the war, some of them to find a living, others to find a refuge from the guillotine of the French Revolution. Some of them burned with a missionary zeal. Others were mere adventurers. But how tell one from the other? These new priests were the chief hope of the new bishop. They had to be. But also they were a chief problem.

Truly, in spite of his thirty-six priests, Bishop Carroll was most lamentably alone. And what does any man alone amount to? He had his own special talents, and his own special nurture of them. He had been sent to Europe at the age of thirteen, and there as a student of the Jesuits, and then as a Jesuit preparing for the priesthood, he had shown that he possessed a scholar's intellect. So much so, that once a priest, ordained to that state in 1759, when he was twenty-four years old, he became a teacher of philosophy and theology at the Jesuit scholasticate at Liège. He was esteemed also as a trainer of the young Jesuits. He had both qualities of leadership and qualities of intellect.

But when he became bishop at the age of fifty-five, what previous experience had he had to train him to be a bishop? He had had some experience of the use of authority simply by being a Carroll in Maryland where even without political rights his family had feudal prestige. Then he had learned something very directly of the variety of peoples that there are on this globe. It must have been awakening for a Marylander to go to school in France, and then in Belgium. When his Jesuit house in Belgium had been confiscated, when his order in France had been suppressed, he had gone travelling through Europe as tutor to the son of a noble Englishman, Lord Stourton. Then after that he had had time to meditate on his travels. He had returned to Maryland and lived and studied for nine years in the private house of his own mother. This retirement had been more than intellectual and spiritual seclusion. There were no real parish churches in Maryland at this time. His mother's chapel had to be a parish church and in it he had to serve as parish priest. He had passed nine years, therefore, as a parish priest, and those years were the trying years of our War of Independence. And it was also during this period that he met the leaders of the Colonial cause in Philadelphia, and that he had enlarged his field of travels by going to Canada, and became conversant with the new, less provincial type of American mind, such as that of Benjamin Franklin. Then he had for three years acted as the Catholic priest in the newly freed nation who directed the other priests. He had the title of Prefect Apostolic. These three years were such as would fit a man to act as bishop. Otherwise by training and by native talents he seemed more fitted to be a schoolmaster.

But Bishop Carroll had no illusions as to his native qualities, nor as to the fitness for his new position that his past experiences had conferred on him. He considered himself, if you will, as a misfit, and most certainly as one faced with a task far above his powers. But what of it?

Salve Regina! Bishop Carroll had had one great spiritual experience in his life : he had lived through the suppression by the Pope, at the insistence of the Bourbon Kings, of his order, the Jesuits. He had foreseen the papal action four years after his ordination, when in 1763 France had expelled the Jesuits, but the full weight of the suppression came as a terrible blow. It was in 1773 when he was visiting with his young ward, Lord Stourton's son, the shrine of Our Lady at Loretto in Italy. He had written to his brother Daniel at the time : "I am not, and perhaps never shall be, recovered from the shock of this dreadful intelligence. The greatest blessing which in my estimation I could receive from God would be immediate death ; but if He deny me this, may His holy and adorable designs on me be wholly fulfilled."

"His holy and adorable designs on me"! And now those "holy and adorable designs" were on him, and in his utter helplessness, could he forget those days at Loretto when he had received news of the Society's suppression? It was not in mere formality that he ordered that the Litany of Loretto be recited in his churches.

Nor was it pure formality that he insisted in his first sermon as bishop that the people of his diocese have a devotion to Our Lady.   It was a sense of his human helplessness, and of all human helplessness.

And it was with the same sense of how little a man's proud important effort can accomplish that he had accepted so gladly — and for us so significantly — the Carmelites as the first religious order to enter the United States.   The useless Carmelites !   They who only pray ; and who pray for the priests, and for the fragility of priests.   The United States had need of Carmelites.

In calling on the Carmelites he was moreover only tapping a strength which had long hiddenly been Maryland's.   Maryland had no Carmel.   She could not in the old days have had one.   But there were Carmels that belonged to that remnant of England's Catholics who had founded Maryland.   They were in Belgium, and one of them, that at Antwerp, had been founded by Lady Mary Lovell Roper, who was a descendant of Saint Thomas More.   The daughters of Maryland had been accustomed to enter these Belgian Carmels.   And now they merely returned from their Belgian exile, headed by a sister who derived from the Carmel founded by the More family. They were four in number, one of them an English girl. On the Feast of the Presentation of Our Lady, 1790, they arrived in New York, and settling at Port Tobacco, Maryland, became a visible sign of the invisible strength which had brought Maryland into being, and which now the son of Maryland, Bishop Carroll, so sorely needed.

There were at this time but five real cities in the United

States. There was Philadelphia with seventy thousand inhabitants, much the richest, much the most luxurious. Then there was New York with sixty thousand. Then came Boston and Baltimore with thirty-five thousand each, and fifth came Charleston, South Carolina. It was necessary that Bishop Carroll establish his authority in all these places. And it was to Boston that he turned his attention first.

It was on All Souls' Day, 1788, that the first Mass had been publicly celebrated in Boston. The celebrant was the Abbé de la Potherie, formerly a chaplain in the French expeditionary force which had come across the Atlantic to the help of the colonists against England. He was a man of ability and some worldly prudence. He had secured the recognition of the Reverend John Carroll, then the Prefect Apostolic, before he attempted to establish himself at Boston. Then he had hired very cannily a church on Boston's School Street, which he could hire very advantageously because this church, originally deeded to French Huguenots, could by the nature of its deed be used only by people of French descent. He was no Huguenot but he was French, and he seized the opportunity offered to him. He also collected together a congregation of Irish and French Catholics and won the favor of the Protestants by his manners and possibly by the fact that he was a fellow-veteran with many of them. After that, he wrote to the Archbishop of Paris asking for vestments. He was showing real energy, but unfortunately the Archbishop of Paris informed the Prefect Apostolic, Carroll, that the Abbé de la Potherie was a suspended priest. Learning of this, the Prefect had only to suspend him on his own account, and the Abbé, who had his courtesy, disappeared from the scene.

In de la Potherie's place the Prefect Carroll had thereupon installed another French priest of winning ways, the Abbé Rousselet. He soon had wind that this Abbé in spite of his affability was not all that a priest should be, but he did not suspend him ; he sent to Boston to work with him a man who was exactly the Abbé's opposite : the Reverend John Thayer. The latter was as zealous as the Abbé was easy-going. He was a Bostonian, who had once been a Congregational minister, and who had been converted to the Catholic Faith during a visit to Rome which he made in 1783 in order to see at first hand the enormities of Catholicism. He had spent thereupon seven years in Europe during which he had become a priest. Then he had turned up in Baltimore just when the Prefect Apostolic Carroll was departing for Europe. there to be consecrated Bishop. To the Bishop-elect he seemed a god-send, and he sent him to Boston with high hopes. Here was a Bostonian to convert Boston !

After his consecration and his return to America, the Bishop found that he had not at all settled the difficulties at Boston by sending the Reverend John Thayer there. In fact, there was a quarrel going on there which required his presence. The quarrel was between the Abbé and his Bostonian colleague. The Bostonian was quite in the right : the Abbé was in the wrong. But the Abbé was wrong with more charm than the Bostonian was right and the congregation took more to the Abbé than they took to the Reverend John Thayer. When the

Bishop withdrew his faculties from the Abbé, the Abbé enticed after him a large part of the congregation and set up a new church of his own.   All this had happened in a place where of all places it was important to start well, and where the congregation was so small that divided it could not exist.   No wonder Bishop Carroll made his first voyage as bishop to Boston.

It was in the spring of 1791 that he arrived there.   He had one pleasant surprise : he was well received by the Protestants.   "It is wonderful," he wrote, "to tell what great civilities have been done me in this town, where, a few years ago, a Popish priest was thought to be the greatest monster in the creation."   He was even invited to dine with the Ancient and Honorable Artillery Company at their annual banquet, and was asked to give thanks at its ending.

All this was all very well but other things made him feel how helpless he was.   The Abenakis of Maine visited him.   Hearing that a bishop was on his way to Boston — they knew what a bishop was for they had seen the bishop of Quebec in their visits to Quebec — they sent their delegates to him, presenting him with a crucifix they had inherited from the Black Robes of old, and begging him for one of his Black Robes of today.

What could he do but with sorrow in his heart, and admiration for their perseverance, promise that he would send them a Black Robe, when there was a Black Robe ?

And what could he do for the one hundred and twenty Irish and French Catholics in Boston, for them and for the one New Englander converted, the Reverend John Thayer ?

He did not have to wean them from Father Rousselet
for that priest had not had the wickedness to wish to
provoke a schism, he had merely continued his wander-
ings which were to lead him to a bed of suffering and
penitence. The bishop had to reconcile the followers
of the departed pastor with their true pastor, Father
Thayer. He accomplished this. He united the one hundred and twenty Catholics under one roof of worship.
Then he had to attend to the details of parishional administration for which Father Thayer was ill suited. He
made arrangements for the payments of debts, even of
those contracted by the Abbé Rousselet. Then he quitted
Boston. But he knew as he quitted the town that he had
really accomplished little. The Reverend John Thayer
(whom I persistently call by that title in order to remind
myself and my readers that in those days ordinary priests
were not called "Father" but simply *Mister*) was a
preacher, a controversialist, an ascetic, a militant Christian, one who had the courage to be a martyr, but not
never, a priest to be pastor to a parish. The Bishop was
to be made aware of this more vividly in the future, but
already he had eyes for this truth. But what could he
do about it? Whom did he have to appoint in his place?
So he left Boston after simply having done a little parish
work on his own account.

His trip to Boston did not make him feel like a lordly
bishop. But his relations with at least three other of the
five cities of his diocese were even more humbling. In
Philadelphia his difficulties were not caused by itinerant
priests of whom he could know little: he was near to
Philadelphia. Nor was it caused by the paucity of the

Catholics and their inability to support a church. It was rather that the Catholics in Philadelphia had been well-treated by the Quakers, and they had begun to flourish without a bishop. Where that happens it is inevitable that some other leaders than bishops take up a bishop's leadership. In Philadelphia these leaders were laymen of two kinds : first those raised up by pride of wealth, such as the trustees of the church of St. Mary's who wished to treat their church as if it were their private property, and second, those who were animated by pride of race, who wished to have their German-speaking Catholic church not under the jurisdiction of this English-speaking Maryland bishop.

With the first kind of pride Bishop Carroll picked no quarrel. He could foresee danger ahead, but he let that danger be met when it arrived as it did — after his own death. With the Germans, however, he was forced into conflict even against his will. He could not help having respect for these German Catholics. They were the spiritual children of his own Jesuit colleagues, who from their German province had come to Pennsylvania in the last half of the eighteenth century and had tended to the Catholic German immigrants. Under the Quaker régime they had been allowed to do some excellent tending ; they had been freer than in Maryland to tend to the poor and to the average man. They had established schools, they had built churches. They were beloved by their flock, and Father Farmer of Philadelphia — to use his Anglicized name — was, except for Father Carroll, the most prominent priest in all the colonies ; and as a missionary who evangelized New Jersey, New York, Delaware, Virginia, he was far more conspicuous. Now the Jesuit order had been suppressed. Now Father Farmer and the old Jesuits were dead, but the Bishop wished to conciliate the new Germans : he took as his first auxiliary bishop a German Father Graessel, and at Philadelphia he allowed the Germans to have a separate church and to choose for it as pastor a Father Helbron of whom he did not approve, but whom he was willing to install among them. But soon they turned against that very pastor, drove him out, and chose another whom the Bishop could not approve of, and whom he had no right to approve of, a Father Goetz. Bishop Carroll was forced to excommunicate Father Goetz. At this the trustees of this church — which had the holy name of Holy Trinity — rejected not only the Bishop's authority but even that of the Pope.

Bishop Carroll was not a hot-head. He was by nature a peacemaker. He visited Philadelphia in 1797 to appease the fraction of Germans who — it should be said — did not represent the real German body of Catholics although they tried to give the impression that they were all the Germans. He approached them as a friend, but scarcely was he within the city than a writ was served on him. He was summoned to court. — Let us turn the page. — For five years Holy Trinity Church remained in schism.

In Baltimore, even in Baltimore, his see city, where he was planning to erect his cathedral, he had so little prestige that a similar indignity was offered to him. Here again the trouble came from among the Germans, but more from a priest who led the malcontents than

from the German laymen. The priest's name was Rue-
ter — not that there is any need of immortalizing the
poor man. — Father Reuter inspired the Germans — only
thirty of whom in the whole city did not speak English
— to build a church, St. John's, and had himself named
by them, against the Bishop's wish, pastor of it. Bishop
Carroll as usual was not drastic in his demands. He was
willing to accept the situation provided only that the
pastor recognized the ecclesiastical jurisdiction which
the Holy Father had conferred on him. The pastor
was reasonable enough to wish to submit, but the trustees of the new church had become so roused by his
previous tirades that when the bishop tried to enter
their church on a January day, 1804, they shut the doors
against him. Only then did he act as the master that
he was. He formally deprived Father Reuter of his
pastorate and put in his place a German of a very different kind, Father Brosius, and then in order to be able
to enforce the appointment, he appealed, as it humili-
ated him so to do, to the civil courts. The courts decided in his favor. His was the victory. But a victory
at what cost !

In New York City no doors were closed to him, and
for a very good reason. They had been so rudely closed
to him as Prefect Apostolic that those who had closed
them to him before he was bishop — that is the lay trustees of St. Peter's Church — were horrified at their own
effrontery. They had barred him from celebrating
Mass at St. Peter's, and had forced him to retire to the
private chapel of the Spanish Consul. This was farther
than they had meant to go. So now they accepted the

priest that he sent them — a Father William O'Brien
Dominican — and by good fortune liked and admired
him.

In Charleston, on the other hand, he was utterly
powerless. A Father Gallagher assumed there a bishop's
power. Father Gallagher was an Irish counterpart of
the Abbé de La Potherie : he was a wandering priest
looking for a place to rule. But he was abler. At
Charleston he began with a dozen Catholics, but soon
unearthed over a hundred others who were too craintive
at first to show themselves. He created a parish where
before the Revolution it had been treason to be a Catholic. He built a church. But, after that, to submit to
a bishop, no.

Charleston was half a thousand miles away, less accessible than Boston. Bishop Carroll did not visit the
city. He sent there in his own place a Father Ryan
but the Catholics, Father Gallagher's sheep, would have
nothing to do with him. Then he sent a Frenchman, the
Abbé Le Moyne. Father Gallagher would not allow
him to celebrate Mass in the Charleston church. When
Bishop Carroll then forbade Father Gallagher himself
to say Mass in it, he persuaded the trustees to order the
church torn down. This was too much for the congregation : they stayed his hand. But the prestige in
Charleston continued to be Father Gallagher's. He remained occupant of the church.

If Bishop Carroll was so helpless in his five large cities
which were at least accessible, and with which he could
communicate, how much more was he helpless to be
a bishop in the country back from the coast, in the small

towns, on the farms, in the settlements beyond the mountains. It was with a sense of his own helplessness that he saw the helplessness of the church throughout the world when, in his lenten pastoral of 1799, he reflected on the horror of European wars, and on the captivity of the Holy Father at the hands of Napoleon.

"O Beloved Brethren! what powerful motives concur to persuade us to devote the acceptable time, the days of salvation now approaching, for obtaining the desirable and salutary objects for which the Apostolic institution of Lent was introduced! We have to solicit for the Church Divine Protection and its freedom from violence and inthralments, for the restoration of peace to all nations, and especially its preservation in these United States, for the deliverance of our venerable Pontiff from his disastrous captivity and his restoration to the free and independent government of the Church, for steadfastness in the faith and unshaken constancy in the ministers of the sanctuary, and of each one of us particularly, amidst all the violent assaults of infidelity and examples of licentiousness and dissolution of manners."

Yet even if time and again he was to feel during his rule as bishop his own human powerlessness, he could not have failed to perceive time and again also evidences of the powerfulness of God in Whose Hands his task was set. Favors came to him beyond his reasonable hope or his farthest planning.

It was not his planning that gave him a seminary at Baltimore. It was the French Revolution. Immediately after his consecration while he was still in England, he received a letter from the Superior of St. Sulpice in

Paris who already saw that France might soon be no place for seminaries, suggesting that a Sulpician Seminary be transplanted to Baltimore.   It was a handsome offer, for the transportation was to cost Bishop Carroll not a cent, and the priests of St. Sulpice once in Baltimore were to train his students for the priesthood gratis, yet far from leaping at the favor, Bishop Carroll was at first skeptical of it.   Finally, however, he accepted it, recognizing it as a favor of Divine Providence : "While I cannot but thank Divine Providence for opening on us such a prospect, I feel great sorrow in the reflection that we owe such a benefit to the distressed state of Religion in France."   So in 1791 there set sail from St. Malo, France, a present from France, four Sulpician priests to act as teachers, each one of whom had been a director of some Sulpician Seminary in France, and four seminarians, of whom two were of English birth, and one an American. In their ship they took with them, as if to launch him off on his literary career, a young man of twenty : Chateaubriand.   Once at Baltimore they launched their projected seminary : the Seminary of St. Mary.

The storm in France swept other blessings to America. There came refugee to our country the Abbé Matignon, who solved for Bishop Carroll all his anxieties concerning Boston.   The Abbé Matignon took over the Reverend Thayer's harassed parish and made it a real parish. And after him came refugee Cheverus and made the parish into a bishopric.   And Father Flaget from France became the first bishop west of the Alleghanies.   And Father Richard became the builder, religious and even temporal, of Detroit.   Without the French Revolution it is hard to see how Bishop Carroll could have got on at all.

But there were other surprises that came to him beyond his planning, which could not be attributed to such an event of general import as the French Revolution. They were isolated, less explicable. There was the Russian, Prince Demetrius Gallitzin. Surely Bishop Carroll never planned to have a Russian prince come as missionary to his scattered sheep in the Alleghany Mountains. When Prince Gallitzin first arrived, he had no way even of recognizing him as a missionary. He was a Russian aristocrat who because of the troublous times was making his world-tour in the New World rather than in the Old. He had with him a learned priest, skilled in higher mathematics, as a tutor, Father Brosius, a German. His mother had become a convert to the Catholic faith, and equipped him with a letter of introduction from the Bishop of Heidelberg to the Bishop of Baltimore. His grandfather, his mother's father, a Prussian general, and a thorough Protestant, had given him a letter to General Washington. The young man himself was a convert like his mother, but his training had been military, and military in a very punctilious, old-world style. Intellectually he appeared to be the last man for any frontier. He had been dandled as a babe in the lap of the skeptical philosopher Diderot. Then after his mother's conversion he had been talking in drawing-rooms with Catholics but with ultra-intellectual Catholics : philosophers, theorists, educators.

After the young Prince Gallitzin, twenty years old, cavalry officer by profession, had been several months in America, he announced to Bishop Carroll that he wished to enter St. Mary's Seminary, Baltimore, and to join the clergy of the United States. Even then the Bishop did not see in him any future missioner. He feared that the young man had some misconceptions concerning the new nation, that he expected to convert some Diderots, in a drawing-room, or to minister to theorizing Catholics in some house like his mother's, and in order to cure him of that illusion, he invited him to accompany him on his visitations for a month or two.

But Prince Gallitzin did become a missionary. He passed through St. Mary's Seminary, and became the second priest to be ordained in the United States. He passed a long life working in western Pennsylvania in the watershed of the Alleghanies, in a region which he called Loretto after the shrine in Italy where Bishop Carroll had had the most heart-piercing moment of his life — though the Prince knew it not. His faithful flock there, and his half-faithful, were everything that he was not. They were untidy, rough in manner, undisciplined, the opposite of book-learned. Yet he changed his name to Smith to be one of them, and set before himself the task of creating a really Catholic community. Trusting to his private wealth, he bought an extent of territory worth one hundred and fifty thousand dollars, and sold it for next to nothing to Catholic settlers. One can imagine some of the trials he had : how he exasperated his flock by his emphasis on cleanliness in his church, how his life was threatened by border ruffians who resented his bringing the Ten Commandments into the wilderness.

One cannot imagine on first thought the real torment of his life : financial troubles.

He had been brought up with a huge fortune and was not used to such anxieties. Even when he became a Catholic priest and was by Russian law, therefore, cut off from inheriting from his father, he did not foresee his difficulties, and went cheerfully ahead : his mother and sisters would back him. But there came a time when mother and sisters could not help, and his life work was about to tumble to the ground through fore- closure of mortgages. He saw himself dragging to ruin, his own Catholic settlers with him. Once under the strain he fainted on the very door-step of Bishop Carroll.

But in the end his scheme prospered. Money came from strange sources, from the King of Belgium whom he had known as a boy. As an old man he became more than a prince, more than a priest, a patriarch, the man of prestige in Pennsylvania's Alleghanies. He could no longer walk. He could no longer — ex-cavalryman — ride. Cheerful as a child in his last winters he was drawn hither and thither on a sled. He was the man of legend. Had he not during the War of 1812 given the militia- company lessons, and had he not fenced with his cane against the militia-captain and his sword and disarmed him again and again ? They had not known he was a prince, and they would have mocked at him if they had known. He was more than prince. What was he ?

But not only from France and from Russia did the presents come. There was a present from England — Father Floyd — who had been converted through the influence of Father John Thayer of Boston. He had come to Baltimore to study with the Sulpicians. Then he had dedicated his life to the poorest at Baltimore, and while he was tending them in a plague of Yellow Fever he caught it. He was a present to Bishop Carroll, not so known to the world as many others. But the Bishop knew him. He had him carried to his own house there to die.

And there were presents from Belgium. There was one priest with the impossible name Father Nerinckx who did much for Kentucky (of whom we shall hear of later). And there were the presents from Ireland. There came from Ireland an Irish Augustinian, Father Rossetter. He had served as an officer of infantry in the French army that had come to the colonies to help Washington. As a priest, when he now returned to America, it was from Washington that he received succor. Fifty dollars came to him from the President to help him to build St. Augustine's Church in Philadelphia.

But surely the most surprising gift from Ireland was not the Augustinians. It was the young Irish girl Alice Lalor ; for it seemed as if literally against her will, against her own Irish bishop's plan, and quite apart from any invitation from Bishop Carroll, she was uprooted by a power above all powers and transplanted from Kilkenny to the District of Columbia, and made to be there the foundress of the Visitandine nuns in the United States. She had come to the United States merely to visit her sister. While there she had felt a call to stay in our country and teach school, but she had promised her bishop in Ireland to return and do the same for him.

He had even given her a ring as a remembrance of her promise. In her noble scrupulosity she would not go back on that promise. Her spiritual adviser in the New World, Father Leonard Neale, could see deeper. "Let me look at the ring." He took it — and utterly mild man that he was — he broke it. It was as if the threads of destiny had to be broken in order that helpless Bishop Carroll might have some help.

Finally, most touching of all was what came to him from the very soil of his own country — his own huge diocese — two religious orders. One had a name from the Old World, *Sisters of Charity*, but she who had founded it had founded it not from any prompting from across the water. She was the most beautiful in appearance of all our converts : she was Elizabeth Seton, the young widow from New York. And her conversion was spiritually even more beautiful. In 1805 she had written in her diary on the Day of the Annunciation — it was a month after her reception into the Church :

"At last God is mine, and I am His. Now let all go its round. I have received Him. — I feel all the powers of my soul held fast by Him who came with so much majesty to take possession of His little poor kingdom. An Easter Communion now, in my green pastures amidst the refreshing fountains for which I thirsted truly." — And the Communion had been received under the gold cross of the St. Peter's Church from which Bishop Carroll had one day not so long before been driven as an outsider. Salve Regina !

The other order which sprang up was also of women. It was the Sisters of Loretto. It must be acknowledged that Father Nerinckx of Belgium was its gardener and planter. Yet it grew on our soil. It sprang up in that county of Kentucky whither the Marylanders — three hundred of them — had trekked in 1773. It derived therefore from Our Lady's old Maryland, and its first superior, Mother Mary Rhodes, was of a Maryland family. And how strange to have here again the name so heart-felt by Bishop Carroll : Loretto ! And the motto of their order was "Love Mary, your loving Mother, sorrowing at the foot of the Cross."

In 1815 Bishop Carroll was on his bed of death. He had been invited to lay the cornerstone of the Washington Monument, for he, eighty years old, was one of the patriarchs who had known Washington, but he was, if not too old, too feeble. It was known by others that he was about to die. It was known by himself.

His task was no more his task. He could not touch it if he would. To him it had never ceased to be a task impossible. Yet something had happened during his performance of it. His diocese was now an archbishopric. There were four bishoprics under him : Boston, New York, Philadelphia, Bardstown. His three million square miles had doubled : the Catholic Church in the United States now included West Louisiana, a district of which the very limits were not known, and Florida. In that territory there were now almost a hundred priests. The number of Catholics were over two hundred thousand, seven times what they had been twenty-five years before. His achievement had been one of the most astounding in the annals of our country, not among those merely of churchmen, but of all men.

Bishop Carroll could well be described as a prosaic man. That is to say whatever temptation there was in him to be lyrical, that he restrained. He moved in the 18th-century manner of the 18th-century gentlemen. He had a classical decorum. On his deathbed he continued to be the prosaic man. Once he heard from the next room some of his priests asking where such and such a book was. It was in fact a book needed in order that he might with proper rites be buried. His thoughts were in the next world, but not so much so that he could neglect his duties in this. He summoned an attendant and whispered the exact information as to where the needed book was : what shelf, and how many volumes from the wall.

Yet his eyes were on the next world, and he could not keep from feeling that if any help had come to him that was unexpected — and he knew it had — it had come to him from an ally he knew well of. His very last request was that he be laid on the floor to die. He was thinking how little he amounted to. Slightly before that, he had spoken to Father Grassi, and he had said in his prosaic way what was a chant of praise :

"Of those things that give me most consolation at the present moment is that I have been always attached to the practise of devotion to the Blessed Virgin, that I have established it among the people under my care, and placed my diocese under her protection."

CHAPTER VIII

THE DELUGE

THEN BEGAN the Deluge. Thirty-eight million foreigners came to our shores during the century that followed the death of Bishop Carroll. No such displacement of population has ever taken place in the world. Over six million Germans came to us, over four million Italians, over three million Poles, and over three million Irish, not to mention the other peoples. We are told that one-eleventh of the population of the globe at this hour is made up of displaced Europeans. Three-fifths of these Europeans are in the United States. We are a country which has had elections, wars, and a most amazing prosperity, but all other countries have had wars; most have had elections, and some have had prosperity. None of these things have made us unique. But we are unique as the receptacle of the greatest displacement of population in the history of the world.

Our country which received this displacement was extraordinarily capable of absorbing it. Its territory was vast, habitable, yet generally uninhabited. Its receiving population had an aptitude for trade and a genius for technical invention, which made it easy to establish almost overnight factories which could use the immigrants as employees. And then the country was so undeveloped in its means of communication that it could use countless arms, and needed to use countless arms, all at once, for building roads over the mountains, for digging canals, for laying railroads. Finally its political system was especially constructed so as to be able to accept men of every race or creed as its citizens. And, finally again, the people already in this nation, those who remembered its founding, had every intention of being pleased by the entrance of newcomers. With an ingenuousness and hopefulness which Dickens found very vulgar, they boasted that God had made our land God's own country, and that they had made it the land of the free, and that therefore it was preferable to every other land. Every newcomer was a compliment to their country and a corroboration of all their boasts. And also they had the philosophy of the philanthropists. They warmed to the thought that they were a refuge to the oppressed.

Yet the suddenness of the torrent was too great for any absorbing. During the Napoleonic wars there had been but little immigration from Europe to the United States. After 1815, after Archbishop Carroll's death, it began to flow in at the rate of some ten thousand a year, and some considered it even in that small volume as worthy of attention : the customs officials were asked in 1820 to count from then on the entering immigrants — suspiciously. But such an immigration prepared no channels for the torrent soon to arrive, nor did it give warning of what it would be like. And the torrent arrived. In the 1840's there were two hundred thousand immigrants arriving annually in our ports. In New York alone would arrive eighty thousand a summer. In the 1850's the total number of immigrants rose to three

hundred thousand a year, one and a half immigrants to
every hundred of the country's population. Thus the
torrent arrived like a cataclysm.

Also the torrent when it arrived was not properly
fluid. It was too poor, too helpless, to flow where it
should. For Europeans to arrive poor on our shores
was no new thing. Of all those who are sometimes
called colonists and not immigrants, who came to our
land before the War of Independence, it was but a
minority that could pay their passage. The Pilgrim
Fathers of Plymouth made themselves as a body indentured servants for seven years in order to pay their way
over on the *Mayflower*. Redemptioners was the name
given to the more usual type of indentured servants who
served a private master individually under bond without wage or with minimum wage, for a certain number
of years in return for having his transportation fee paid
for him. These redemptioners were very numerous, a
fourth of the population surely. And some of them
were men not only of virtue but of training and education, — schoolmasters arrived as redemptioners. But they
were all poor. And likewise the felons who arrived and
had been given free transportation and good riddance
were poor, and they were even more numerous. Benjamin Franklin said that only eighty thousand colonists
crossed the ocean to the English settlements — I think he
was wrong but he said it. — And historians now calculate
that at least fifty thousand felons were transported to our
shores. Such calculations make us realize how very few
must have been those who arrived in our land well-to-do.
No, these immigrants of the Deluge were not the first

to arrive on our shores poor. But their poverty was more helpless. In the old days the poor had arrived with a status, even though that status was often lamentable. They were assimilated into the economic order before they arrived. In the newer times the immigrants had to find their status. They were free and equal and no one was responsible for them. They were responsible for themselves, and could if they would do everything for themselves by working with nothing from nothing.

Many of the immigrants arrived penniless on our shores simply because they had been penniless on the shores from which they started. England sent over many occupants of her poorhouses, which aroused some hostile comment in the United States, like that in *Niles' Weekly Register*, July 3, 1830: "Infamous conduct! The ship *Anacreon* arrived at Norfolk last week from Liverpool, with 168 passengers, three-fourths of whom were transported English paupers, cast on our shores, at about four pounds, ten shillings a head, to get rid of the cost of maintaining them! And a great part of these are from 50 to 60 years of age — some older! Charity will give some of these a passage to Baltimore and we undertake to say that we shall support at least thirty of this cargo of live stock in our poorhouse next winter to relieve British agriculturists of the burden of keeping them."

The Irish, who during the famine years of the later forties were the largest wave of immigrants, coming then at the rate of a hundred thousand a year — a million in ten years — were not the occupants of poorhouses. Ireland was not rich enough to have poorhouses. They came from their own poverty-stricken houses, but they were for the most part utterly penniless, their passage-money often having been paid by charitable societies in Ireland or by fore-runners in America. They were poorer than the English, too, because they had more numerous children to provide for.

Concerning the German immigrants, the United States Consul at Hesse Cassel wrote in 1836 an informative paragraph. He was trying to explain why so many German immigrants arrived in America helpless :

"The great number of German paupers arises from the low rate of passage-money which of late had existed. Steerage passengers were taken last spring from Bremen, and found with good provisions, at $16 each grown person. This price the Bremen shipowners could only afford by carrying always a large number, to obtain which they had their agents all over the interior of Germany, and induced the lower class, which live in a very impoverished state, to emigrate, by making them believe that labor was so much demanded in the United States that any able-bodied man could earn, as soon as landed, $2 a day."

Even if an immigrant had a fair sum of money when he began to think of emigrating from Germany, England or Ireland, it was almost impossible for him to arrive with it in New York. There were too many ways in which he could be mulcted of what he had. Frequently he would buy a ticket of passage from some one who pretended to be agent of this or that company of transport and who would abscond with the payment. — And how was he to know the true agent from the false ?

— Once on the ship, there was a method of extorting his remaining funds. The following was a favorite piece of trickery : the man and his family would be told that the voyage would last but three weeks — let him bring a store of provisions for that period. When the voyage lasted longer than that (I am speaking of the days of sailing ships), and it usually did so last, then the man had to buy provisions from the captain who would charge for them four times their real value.

Sometimes there was terrible starvation. A shipload of Germans had a pitiful time in 1805. They came in the *General Wayne* which though it bore the name of an American general was probably in ownership not American, for in passing on its way from Hamburg to the New World, it forced some of its men passengers ashore at Liverpool to serve in the English army against Napoleon. Then the woes of the passengers really began. The account of them is contained in the records of the German Society of Philadelphia :

"The hunger was so great on board that all the bones about the ship were hunted up by them and pounded with a hammer and eaten : and what is more lamentable, some of the deceased persons, not many hours before their death, crawled on their hands and feet to the captain and begged him, for God's sake, to give them a mouthful of bread or a drop of water to keep them from perishing, but their supplications were in vain ; he most obstinately refused, and thus did they perish. The cry of the children for bread was . . . so great that it would be impossible for man to describe it, nor can the passengers believe that any other person excepting Captain Conklin would be found whose heart would not have melted with compassion to hear those little inoffensive ones cry for bread."

Later there were fewer cases of starvation but more of overcrowding. In 1834 *Niles' Weekly Register* tells of the ship *Thomas Gelston*, which sailed from Londonderry to Montreal, Canada : "The passengers by this vessel state the number, including children, to have been somewhere from 450 to 517. They were nine weeks on the passage, and suffered much from want of water and provisions. Besides two tiers of berths on the sides, the vessel was filled with rows of berths down the centre, between which and the side berths there was only a passage of about three feet. The passengers were thus obliged to eat in their berths, each of which contained a great many persons, say five and upwards. In one were a man, his wife, his sister and five children ; in another were six full-grown young women, while that above them contained five men, and the next eight men."

The overcrowding and the starvation resulted in pestilence, and the ships of immigrants came to be known as fever-ships. We know some of the victims of these fever-ships. We know that Mother Seton's father, as a New York physician, died attending to one such ship. But we easily forget in thinking of the Deluge the fair portion of it that started for our shores yet never arrived. And we lose a true sense of what it all meant by not picturing often enough to our minds the misery of those immigrants who, though they did arrive, arrived as skeletons on our shores, too emaciated to dare to look at themselves in a mirror, too heart-broken to dare to look back at the faces of their family — five, six or a dozen, all of whom they had to throw into the wave.

But suppose the immigrant arrived well and with some money left at New York. Even then he was not safe. There was no special landing place for immigrants till 1855 and before that, no sooner had he come to dock, than he was accosted by sharpers. If he were Irish they talked with a brogue more Irish than he. They took off his bags and bedding as if they were his best friends, led him to a boarding house which was a den of thieves and a counter of misinformation. As a result it was all too natural that thus seventy-five per cent of the English and Irish immigrants found it impossible to go beyond their port of entry, no matter what their plans had been. Into the cities, where they piled up like a procession that arrives at barred gates, they brought the misery which they had left in Europe, accentuated by the further misery acquired in their voyage. They were glad to have arrived where they were. Enough of their companions, not always the best, had made fortunes swiftly enough to convince them that they were in a land of promise — and they were. Even those who made no fortune, but only low wages, made wages fabulous in comparison with wages at home. Yet in comparison with the Americans of the older immigrations they were as a whole a people of misfortune. They were forced into slums to live, and they bore the mark of the slums. They were contumeliously regarded, in a land where wealth was considered the mark of Divine Favor, as somewhat reprobate and therefore and perforce outsiders.

In regard to entering the political life of the community they were also at a disadvantage. Our political system had its general aspect, its theoretical re-foundation after the Revolution, but it remained in practice odd and English, something one had to be apprenticed in to know. Two-thirds of the inhabitants of the central Atlantic States in the pre-Revolutionary days may not have been English but it was the English political traditions that had swallowed the entire early population. The Irish who arrived after the Revolution had their oddness, but it was not an English oddness, and they had no desire to be odd in an English way. There was a difficulty here which even such a lover of abstract theory as Thomas Jefferson pointed out very forcibly. In his notes on Virginia he was willing to remark : "Every species of government has its specific principles. Ours perhaps are more peculiar than those of any other in the Universe." All that gave to the immigrant an equality with the more fortunate who were accustomed to the system, was his vote, and his vote was so valuable that it was coveted by the demagogues, and if possible stolen by them.

Thus the flood of immigration, although it came to a land fitted better than others to absorb it, could not be — not at first at least — absorbed ; and it remained a flood, like a too great rain, or a fertility-giving torrent which begins by causing destruction. Those who had been in the land before it made every effort to rise above it, and looked on it, in spite of any phrases in the Declaration of Independence, as composed of their inferiors. This had its absurdity. Taken as a whole there were much fewer utterly worthless persons in the Deluge of the

'40's and '50's than in the colonial transportations. And it was something of a betrayal of our profession of principles to look down on fellowmen. Yet it was in accord with our old Anglo-Saxon practice of treating the Indians as vermin, and of regarding people who did not do things exactly like us — the Spaniards for instance — as unentitled to fair play. And also it was in accord with one self-evident truth : the older-comers were initiated into the new nation ; the others were not.

The truth is, the people who greeted the immigrants, or who shrank from them, had that xenophobia which no nation ever has been free from. All peoples have their xenophobia and it twines about their virtues, and I do not remember that any reformer has been able to eradicate it without exterminating a people. In fact, xenophobia is the mark of this mortal life of ours, and the greatest difference between our life now and that which we pray to have in Heaven is that in Heaven we shall be in the bottom of our heart unfeignedly happier for every newcomer at Heaven's feast.

Xenophobia, however, if it cannot be eradicated, can be controlled, provided it be called by its right name and properly treated, but this particular xenophobia, that of the citizens of the United States in the first half of the nineteenth century, refused to call itself a xenophobia — it was too proud. It took on a higher motive, pretended to a religious indignation, an anti-Catholicism. It called this flood of indigence and misery the Catholic Church.

And one thing is true : the Catholic Church did not try to float above it. It became gladly drowned in it. Such was in accord with its eternal vocation. The

Church is much more afraid of a high-brow than an illiterate, of a man in soft garments than of one in rags.
Its affinity is perpetually with any misery. And then it
happened that this particular misery was largely a Catholic misery. Not all the immigrants were Catholic, but
half of them were, and those who were most indigent,
most alien among aliens, were Catholics. No land was
stranger for any immigrant, unless he was financier or
Puritan, than Boston. It was a place of one type of
man, one type of discipline, one way of being grim and
thrifty and successful. It was, in more than a religious
sense of the word, the most un-Catholic place in the
universe. Yet into this unhospitable ground came freak-
ish immigration. One can read about it in Catholic
statistics. In 1790 there had been one hundred and
twenty Catholics in Boston. In 1820 there were two
thousand. Then there commenced a trickle : there were
seven thousand in 1828. Then the full Deluge : there
were forty thousand in 1850. And all these Catholics
were Irish and all were immigrants. No wonder the
Church and the immigrants were looked on as one in
and about Boston.

And what was true of Boston was true of other places.
The influx of Catholics was astounding in other New
England cities. In the diocese of Hartford, Connecticut,
in 1854 there were twenty thousand Catholics ; the very
next year there were forty thousand. And there were
cities in the Mississippi Valley where a like increase took
place : in Cincinnati's diocese in 1843 there were fifty
thousand Catholics ; three years later were one hundred
thousand. In 1845 the entire number of Catholics had

been little over one million. During the next ten years a million and a quarter Catholics arrived from Ireland alone, not to mention those from Germany. The Catholics who were not immigrants became a small minority in this great mass, and became undistinguishable from it. The problem of the Church was with the immigrants. And the obsessing work of the clergy was for them. Merely to house them under some kind of a roof where they could hear Mass of Sundays was a task which made other tasks a distraction. And then there were the schools to build, and the hospitals, and the orphanages — all without money.

Even the bishops disappeared in the Deluge ; from any national gaze drowned. Archbishop Carroll had been known far and wide. Bishop Cheverus at Boston was a conspicuous figure in Boston to Protestants as well as Catholics : he belonged to the city. But that was before the Deluge. After the Deluge the bishops belonged to the immigrants and were to the Protestants anonymous. Bishop Fenwick who succeeded Bishop Cheverus at Boston was himself no immigrant — much less than his predecessor. He was a Catholic Marylander of a Catholic Maryland family which had not the wealth of the Carrolls but all their American tradition and prestige. He was as learned a man as Archbishop Carroll, and even more imposing. Yet who in Boston except the Catholics ever heard of him ? He had to play the schoolmaster in a church crypt to the utterly ignorant. He was of the poor, for the poor. There were only two bishops who were widely known in the United States in the days of the Deluge, in its first flood. And one of them was

known because he stood outside of it ; he was Bishop
England of Charleston, in which city there arrived no
immigration : the other was Archbishop Hughes of New
York, and he was known because the flood at New York
was so prodigious that it made him known. He was
the ruler of that flood. I might, if it did not sound dis-
respectful, liken him to a kind of Neptune who rode
on its waves, who quelled the storms, who was loved
by the waves, who was great by them.

There was some logic, therefore, in identifying the
Catholic Church at this time and place with immigrants,
with people generally poor and often unlettered, and
who did not live according to the customs (good or bad)
established in the land to which they came. But really
the confusion of the Catholic Church with foreigners
had nothing to do with logic at all. During the war of
1812 President Madison had decreed a day of fasting
and prayer, because of the disasters our country was en-
during in the capture of her capital, and the dangers
which she faced. At this time there was no immigration whatsoever, much less a Catholic tide of it, yet many
of the Protestant pulpits on that fast day thundered
against the Catholic Church. There was a great atavistic
anti-Catholic emotion pent up in Protestant pulpits which
with or without logic looked for an occasion to vent
itself.

Thus in the early days of the Deluge there came into
being an anti-Catholic movement which gave the motive
power and the ardor to the respectably titled Native
American Movement. It resulted in various riots and
burnings of Catholic buildings, notably in Boston and

Philadelphia. It was, after a manner, a persecution, but, as such, it could not be compared with the great persecutions of history. It had one mania, however, that gives it an unsavory importance. It chose, as its chief mania, a rage against the cult of the Blessed Virgin and against nuns, who were and are her image. When in 1834 the Native American mob burned a Catholic building in Boston, it was not the Cathedral of the Holy Cross that they chose to burn : it was a nunnery — the Ursuline Convent in Charlestown. Ten years afterwards the rioting broke out in Philadelphia. The first cry of the Native Americans as they stood outside of St. Michael's Church was, "Down with the Irish." But the next cry was, "To the Nunnery, to the Nunnery !" They burned down one convent and would have burned down another, had some defenders not fired a warning shot at them. Two churches, one of them St. Michael's, the other St. Augustine's, to which Washington had given $50, were also burned to the ground, and those who were there say that the shout which went up from the crowd when the gold cross of St. Augustine's began to topple into the flames was like the shout of Hell, yet even then more fiendish, more blood-curdling, more particularly sinister, was the poor misguided cry : "To the Nunnery, to the Nunnery !"

Some people may ask how this perversity came about. Whence this madness ? It is not for me to explain, but those who ask should read some of the writings of these days of the Deluge. Even some respectable Protestant ministers were responsible for the mania. In the 1820's and '30's there was a very conspicuous Presbyterian minister who entered into various controversies with Father Hughes of Philadelphia, later to be Bishop Hughes of New York. His name was the Reverend R. J. Breckenridge. Look on page 59 of his book entitled *Papism in the 19th Century*, published in 1826, and see his horror at finding in the Baltimore Cathedral, newly completed, such honor paid to Our Lady. He noticed, as if he were a spy seeing what no one else could see, that the magic letters A.M. were behind the Bishop's chair. So he concluded, "All these altars, this edifice, the ecclesiastics who officiate here, all in short, it thus appears are devoted to the worship and care of a pious Jewish female, who about eighteen centuries ago, after fulfilling her singular and glorious destiny in this world returned again, as to her mortal part, to the earth as it was, and as to her soul, to God who gave it."

The Reverend Breckenridge was the most respectable of the shouters-out against "Mariolatry" and nuns, and it cannot but be perceived that in his rage he almost melts into reverence when he really finds himself obliged to define what Our Lady was. We can have a soft spot for some of his words : they were true. He at least perceived that Baltimore was dedicated to Our Lady.

But he was much more respectable than the others. He may have roused some rioters, but those who cried out "To the Nunnery," had been roused by writings stronger than his : by the pornographic literature which pretended to be revelations of what went on in convents. The most famous of these books was *The Revelations of Maria Monk*, her *Awful Disclosures*.

It is not to bicker over an incident much better forgotten that I revive mention of such a book. It is not to stain the name of Maria Monk's backers, some of whom were merely miseducated men who were honorable enough at last to acknowledge their error — after the harm was done. Nor is it to revive the unfortunate chapter in the history of a New York publishing house, which in name still exists, and which published the book, knowing it to be a fraud, under the assumed name of Howe & Bates. The incident is one which explains a whole fifty years of our country's history, and takes us to the reading book of a million families in the 1830's when a million families was a considerable proportion of all the families in our land. Eighty thousand copies of the book were sold within a year, and three hundred thousand and more in a decade. The *Awful Disclosures* made American history as Harriet Beecher Stowe's *Uncle Tom's Cabin* did.

But Harriet Beecher Stowe was trying to tell the truth ; Maria Monk was trying to tell anything but the truth. The truth was that she was a very pitiable prostitute who had been put by her mother in a Magdalen asylum in Montreal, from which she had escaped. The rest of the story arouses terrible laughter, dry as the crackling of dried sticks. The Reverend Lyman Beecher, uncle of Harriet Beecher Stowe, was at this time trying to rouse the country against the menace of Catholicism. This time was in 1835. One of the well-meaning members of Protestant ministry in Canada was indeed aroused. He organized a society "designated to arrest the progress of Popery and to enlighten and convert their ignorant, vicious and degraded subjects." The prostitute, Maria Monk, must have thought very little of this minister's brains, and much of his credulity. She somehow met him and told him that she had been five years a novice and two years a Blue Nun at the Hôtel Dieu at Montreal, and then she told him of the disclosures which aroused his indignation. He saw to it that the disclosures were printed at New York, first in a magazine, *The Protestant Vindicator*. Maria was invited into Protestant drawing-rooms where her behavior was seldom decorous, to say the least, but that was, so it was explained, because she was a nun or had once been a nun. Furthermore, she could not express herself in language such as the polite were used to, but that was easily remedied: a very polished man, Theodore Dwight, nephew of Yale's President, acted as her "shadow writer," and no one was the wiser. It was her facts, so Dwight thought, that were important. Where is there a more terrible subject for a satiric comedy than this career of Maria Monk? The only trouble is that it is too terrible.

Then came the catastrophe, equally ironic. The disclosure of the author of the *Awful Disclosures* began not grandly, but in greed. There was a quarrel about the profits of the book. The minister who had discovered Maria, a certain Reverend William K. Hoyt, sued the Reverend T. T. Slocum and Maria Monk for his share of the royalties, and the two defendants would have had to go off to jail together, had not bail of $5000 been forthcoming. Shortly after that the ministers were able to acknowledge that Maria was not at all what they had thought her to be.

All this is very comic, but the results were tragic. The *Awful Disclosures* continued to sell, and to be believed. It is still sold. The Catholic immigrants arrived here among people who believed in the disclosures, and in other disclosures. They were made to suffer for their Church simply by being known to belong to such a corrupt institution. They were by definition those whom Maria Monk's first patron had dedicated himself and herself to redeem : "the ignorant, vicious and degraded subjects" of Rome.

The anti-Catholic riots of the 1830's were a disgrace, yet they served two good purposes. They disclosed first that this talk about Native Americanism being the exclusive property of the Protestants was nonsense. During the riots the record of the Catholics was utterly admirable ; they were behaving like Americans. In Philadelphia it was not the Catholics but the anti-Catholics who knocked the mayor of the town senseless. It was with a recognizably American voice that Bishop Kenrick after two days of rioting had addressed a letter to his flock :

To the Catholics of the City and County of Philadelphia :

Beloved children : In the critical circumstances in which you are placed, I feel it my duty to suspend the exercises of public worship in the Catholic churches which still remain, until it can be resumed with safety, and we can enjoy our constitutional right to worship God according to the dictates of our conscience. I earnestly conjure you to practice unalterable patience under the trials to which it has pleased Divine Providence to subject you ; and remember that affliction will serve to purify us, and render us acceptable to God, through Jesus Christ, who patiently suffered the cross.

✠ Francis Patrick
Bishop of Philadelphia

May 10, 1844.

As for the leaders of the Native Americans in the riotings, they were not even by birth Americans. Some of them were Italian atheists. The great leader in Philadelphia was an Irish ex-priest — Hogan. The leader who was leader almost everywhere called himself the Angel Gabriel. He rode on a white horse attired in flowing white garments. He carried no birth-certificate with him (his real name was Orr), yet I doubt if he was born in Heaven, and I hope he was not born anywhere in the United States.

The other good turn that the rioting did and the general persecution that attended it, was that it identified the Catholics with a loyalty to the Blessed Virgin. It defined them as "Mariolaters," as defenders of nuns, as believers in the Incarnation, and in the mystery of a supernatural vocation. It conferred an honor on them. It separated the Church in our land from any danger it may have had of thinking that the Christian faith was but a way of thought, a plausible opinion, a philosophy which many wise men had held. No, it was something to make us children. We began by being the shepherds who were the first to visit the new-born Christ, even before the wise men. We were not Catholics for any reason merely civic : we were Catholics in order to be able to have the privilege to say the rosary, and to kneel before the statue of Our Lady, and to kiss with our lips, which any immigrant amongst us had, the straw of the crib on Christmas day. We had a Church not founded on, not even buttressed by, any pride in our own talents.

In 1846, not long after the Native American riots, there met in Baltimore the sixth provincial council. While it was meeting, the armies of the United States were entering New Mexico and California. We were taking over more lands which the Spaniards had dedicated to the Immaculate Conception. Those in the council were not thinking about these invading armies. They had no way of knowing even whether they were conquering or being conquered. Yet they seemed unconsciously in one act of theirs to be preparing our land to take over Spain's old responsibilities. Twenty years of the Deluge had tightened the bond between the Church in our country and the Mother of God. It was a spontaneous act, therefore, when, in this council, permission was sought from Rome that we be allowed to elect as our patroness, her, who to the immigrants was not only their life, their sweetness and their hope, but also their only true equality, only true liberty, only true fraternity, the "Blessed Virgin Conceived Without Sin."

CHAPTER IX

FATHER DE SMET

IT IS a fact well known, but not often meditated upon, that practically every part of our country began by having a Catholic history. That history was in every case what the world would call the story of a failure. In 1840 there still remained one portion of our country — call it a fourth — which was void of any history, failure or success — the Northwest. In the early eighteenth century a French-Canadian, La Verendrye, had voyaged to Montana. Later the Spanish had gone up as far as the Mandans on the Missouri River, into the Dakotas. And Lewis and Clark, sent by President Jefferson, had gone farther even than the Spanish and the French. They had gone clean to Oregon's coast overland. Also there had been numerous trappers who had gone into this region overland, and also the fur-traders had visited Oregon by sea and started the fortune of the Astors. Yet this was not history, not, at least, history of the Northwest, but only of visitors to it. The first history of this region was to be a Catholic history. It was to be the story of the plans of a very unique missionary, a Belgian Jesuit, Father De Smet.

Father De Smet was an example of the teeming, vigorous life of Catholic Belgium which had not been interrupted as France's and Spain's Catholic life had been by the French Revolution. His father was a Belgian burgher vigor personified. He was a citizen of Termonde, who after having been the father of ten children by his first marriage, married a second time at fifty-seven and became the father of nine more children. The fifth of the latter group was Pierre De Smet, who was to make the Catholic history of the Northwest. Although born of an ageing father he had all the vigor his father ever had, and more too. As a schoolboy he was nicknamed by his fellow-students, "Samson," because of his great strength. He was overflowing with lustiness, and he continued always to be overflowing with lustiness. As he wrote to a niece of his, when he was a missionary, he had a mouth given mostly to laughter and to making others laugh.

Pierre De Smet, without ceasing to be a good laugher and an unshorn Samson, had a God-given sense of the heroic, and he decided to become a priest, and if possible a missionary. While he was studying for the priesthood he met Father Nerinckx who had been living in Kentucky at the ends of the earth. This missionary was not a Jesuit (possibly only because the Jesuit order had been in its state of suppression during his youth), but he was a great recruiter for the Jesuits, and his enthusiasm for a life in the United States was so contagious that young Pierre De Smet decided to become both a Jesuit and a Jesuit missionary in the United States, in some wild portion of it, preferably among the Indians. This made his hard-headed father think that his son was becoming a trifle romantic, and he did his best to dissuade him from anything precipitate. Yet precipitately, at the age of seventeen, he managed on the Feast of the Assumption in

1821 to sail for the United States in an American ship, the *Columbia*. Forty-two days later he arrived at Philadelphia, was disappointed not to find it a wilderness, but a city like European cities, and thereupon proceeded to Whitemarsh, the Jesuit novitiate not far from Washington, D.C.

The next year his travels toward the wilder lands began. He walked with eleven other Jesuit pupils, ten of them Belgians like himself, the other one an American, over the Alleghanies, escorting two wagons of their baggage and supplies. He was being sent with the others to found a Jesuit province in Missouri, at Florissant, near St. Louis. It was a six weeks' journey, first over the mountains afoot, then down the Ohio in two little boats that they tied together. Then up the banks of the Mississippi afoot to the Missouri mouth, leaving their baggage to be carried by the wonder of wonders, the steamboat. After such a journey it must have seemed to him that he would arrive beyond the range of White Men, and he knew that one reason why he was going so far was that the United States government had offered to subsidize an Indian school if the Jesuits would man it. And the Jesuits had seized the opportunity as a help to them in establishing a western province for themselves in the scene of their old labors before the suppression of their order : the French Mississippi Valley. Yet Florissant, which was on the north bank of the Missouri above St. Louis, was already, before he came there, becoming a White Man's town. Even some Sisters of the Sacred Heart were there from France, making it like Old France. He did come upon Indians, and he taught them while waiting to be ordained, but his eyes were always to the west, to Indians who were even more Indian-like.

It seemed to him useless to try to make the White Men holy unless the White Men paid first their debt to the Indians. The bad treatment of the Indians had been the one great crime of the new nation. He knew well it had robbed them of their lands, time and again, even after solemn treaties. He knew also how the frontiersmen had debauched the Indians, for he saw the Indians with the mark of the White Men upon them. He was obsessed with the idea of going to the help of the Red Men who were wronged, of living for them. "Believe me," he said to Mother Duchesne of the Order of the Sacred Heart at Florissant, "Believe me, you will never succeed in this country unless you call down the blessing of Heaven by founding schools for the Indians."

It was not till 1840, till he was thirty-six, that he really began his life-work by going beyond the lands where the White Men were dominant. Then suddenly his prayers began to be answered, and significantly it was the Indians who came to seek him, rather than he who sought them. I have already spoken of the Flat Head Indians of the Rocky Mountains in Montana. It was they who had come four times to St. Louis asking for a Black Robe. On their last visit they were allowed to have Father De Smet. They had earned him by their perseverance, and he had earned them by his constant longing to go, missionary, to the farthest regions, to Indians who were still absolutely Indians and uncontaminated by frontier life.

He started from St. Louis in March 1840, went up the Missouri by boat to Westport, now Kansas City, from which place the caravan routes to Santa Fé and Oregon had their point of departure. He was accompanied by one Indian, the young Ignatius, an Iroquois who had become an adopted member of the Flat Head Tribe, and who spoke French. He bought a horse to carry his own two hundred and ten pounds, and a horse for Ignatius and five other horses beside. He joined a caravan of the American Fur Company. Off they rode.

This first voyage toward the Rockies gave him a foretaste of his forty years of future labors and of his success in them and of the blessing that was to be upon them. He began by putting all his journeyings under the protection of Our Lady, for he was what the world would call childish in his devotion to her. Without her he could and would do nothing, any more than Father Marquette. Then he fell sick of a fever, and he had to be stowed in a supply-wagon. The plains over which they moved was cut with gullies which caused the wagon to ride at times bow-down like a small boat in a rough sea, or vice versa. I do not know that this amused him at the moment. But in retrospect he was gleeful over the singular figure that he cut. "At one instant I was feet in air, the next I disappeared in the bales and crates."

By mid-May he had come to the Platte River, the river too shallow to navigate and therefore entitled to the term applied to it of the "most useless of rivers," and yet as a land-mark so indispensable : it guided the caravans over the plains to the South Pass, the gate-way through the Rockies. He was not over his fever, but he and his two hundred and ten pounds were again astride of a horse. He was miles from nowhere and he breathed the free-

dom of the open air into his lungs, and he began to specu-
late. He played the prophet. This is what he wrote
down :

"Perhaps this country will be some day the cradle of a
new people, composed of the ancient savage races and of
that class of adventurers, fugitives, and outlaws, which society casts off : a population heterogeneous and threaten-
ing, which the American Union pushes ahead of it as a
sinister cloud on its frontiers, and the size of which it always increases, and the irritation of it also, as it transports
whole tribes of Indians from east of the Mississippi to the
solitudes of the West. These savages carry along with
them an implacable hatred of the Whites who, they say,
have unjustly driven them from the tombs of their fathers
and dispossessed them of their heritage. Is it not to be
feared that with the passage of time these tribes may or-
ganize themselves into bands of robbers and murderers,
who can profit by the light courser-like horses of the
prairie, who can use the desert as the theatre of their
brigandage and the inaccessible rocks as the refuge and
fortress for them and their booty ?"

On the last day of June he arrived at the Green River,
a branch of the Colorado, and there he came face to face
with the Indians who had called him to them : the Flat
Heads. In their simple gratitude and expectancy they
had come eight hundred miles to meet him.

With them, wonder of wonders, was one of his own
people — a Belgian, Jean-Baptiste De Velder. Conscripted
as a boy by Napoleon, he had fought for Napoleon in
Spain, and there, made prisoner, had continued his adventures by escaping on an American ship. Now De Velder

was one of the fur-traders who had lived in the northwest of our country for twenty years, ever among Indians. He had almost forgotten his native tongue, re-
taining it only in his remembered prayers — which he
seldom said — and in a hymn to Our Lady which he had
learned from his mother before he could walk. Father
De Smet revived the Christian that still smouldered in De
Velder, and made of Napoleon's grenadier, turned fur-
trader, a most faithful, loving and useful aide-de-camp.

With De Velder, Father De Smet quitted the caravan
of the American Fur Company and became one of the
Flat Head Indians. It was not difficult to make himself
at home among them. They had longed for a Black Robe
for twenty years and now at last they had found one.
And he himself had all his life long dreamed of meeting
just such Indians as these — who would come eight hundred miles in Indian courtesy and noble hope. — It was a
dream : he knew it was a dream while he was dreaming it.
And yet now he was awake and it was true. So he knew
these Indians like old friends. "I wept with joy," he
said, "in embracing them."

Embracing them. The love was not all from him to
them. Their filial affection frightened him by its trustfulness. The aged wrinkled chiefs, patriarchs, wanted
to be children to him — and he only thirty-six. Every
word of his they remembered. Words were still a treasure to them, a wisdom. It was dangerous to speak lightly.
They forced him to preach to them four times a day.
The day after he arrived he translated for them into their
tongue with the aid of an interpreter the prayers that it
was best for them to know. Two weeks later he held up

a medal of Our Lady, and promised it to the first who could recite "the Pater, the Ave, the Credo, the ten commandments and the four acts" of faith, contrition, hope and love., An aged chief stood up. "Give it to me." He knew the prayers and acts word for word, and, wearing Our Lady's medal, was appointed the catechist of the tribe.

What a land De Smet marched through with these Indians! It was a country of proud sky-touching mountains, superb Christmas-tree forests, streams pure as if they poured from Heaven. There was the thunder of the stream, the roar of the wind, but the silence of the edge of the world. In the seventeenth century the Jesuits had seemed to have as little sense of natural scenery as Racine had had. Father De Smet belonged to a different age. He had read and he sometimes quoted Chateaubriand. He was a painter in his heart like many a Fleming. Through sunsets and snowy mountains, and along torrents, and under the night of the great fir trees he proceeded northward, and then swinging east across the mountains toward the headwaters of the Missouri came to the Yellowstone River. He was not going to visit the home valley of the Flat Heads this year. That was farther north, and the season was growing late. Farewell to the Flat Heads.

Farewell to the Flat Heads, and au revoir. And before he took leave of them he consented to baptize three hundred of them. There were two thousand in the tribe; they all wanted baptism. But no. Not yet. Not all of them. And he would be back. He had been ordered by the chief of the Black Robes to return to St.

Louis and report on what he had seen, and he had to obey orders. But next year he would be back, and he would come to their valley on the Clark River, to their green cleft in the Great Divide, and he would then build a chapel for them, and round that chapel establish a reduction for them, a heaven on earth. Did he not want an escort on his way home ? No, the Flat Heads had better not venture among the Black Feet and other Sioux tribes of the Upper Missouri and the Great Plain, for such were their overwhelming and inveterate enemies. He would go from them alone, taking with him only his Napoleonic grenadier, De Velder. Au revoir.

Au revoir. The Indians had their own way of saying au revoir. "Adieu," they cried to him. "Black Robe, may the Great Spirit accompany you. Evening and morning we shall offer our supplications for you, that you may arrive safe and sound among your brothers at Saint Louis. We shall continue to make our prayers for you until you return to us your children of the Mountains. When, after the winter, the snow shall disappear from the valleys, and the greenness of things shall have rebirth, our hearts at this time so sad will recommence to rejoice. And as higher and higher grows the grass, so greater and greater will grow our joy. And when the buds shall once again break into flower, we shall go forth again once more to our meeting with you. Black Robe, adieu."

It was September now. Father De Smet and his grenadier were sleeping at night under the stars. There was danger from Indians, danger from wild animals. They had horses with them, and a compass. According to Father De Smet the grenadier was the braver of the two. He never stayed sleepless ; he slept at touching his head to the earth, and he snored. He snored, said Father De Smet, like a steam engine (which in those days snored more terribly than now). It was difficult for Father De Smet to get to sleep.

But fatigue, as he went on, blessed him with nightly sleep. He came to the outposts of the Fur Company on the Missouri, Forts Union, then Clark, then Pierre. A French-Canadian trapper joined them.

One day while they were crouching in a ravine as they stole through the country of the Sioux, a band — the Black Feet of the Plain — came upon them, mounted, armed, and ferociously naked.

Let Father De Smet describe the Dantesque dialogue :

"Thereupon, I rose and presented my hand to the one who appeared to be the chief. 'Why do you hide in this ravine ?' he said to me coldly. 'Are you afraid of us ?' 'We were hungry,' I replied. 'The spring here invited us to take a rest.' "

At this the chief studied the Black Robe from head to foot, showing particular interest in the cross the Father wore. Then he turned to the Canadian :

"Never in my life have I seen a man of this kind. Who is he ? Whence comes he ?"

Then, according to Father De Smet, the Canadian did not economize the attributes and titles he conferred on him :

"He is the man who speaks to the Great Spirit. He is the Black Robe of the French ; he has come to visit the many Indian tribes."

"The Black Robe of the French," was the Canadian's way of putting it. A century back these Sioux had known the Black Robes of the French. De Smet was their successor, and he was one who profited by them. He belonged with them to a one errand of mercy. — "The Black Robe of the French !"

At this the chief became mild and amicable. He told his warriors to put down their arms, exchanged courtesies with the Black Robe, and the peace pipe was smoked.

The honors accorded to De Smet were even startling. He was invited to sit down on a buffalo robe — an invitation not at all extraordinary, and quite appropriate to a weary traveler. — Father De Smet accepted the honor, and then, to his amazement, found that the Sioux warriors had seized it by its corners and were carrying him and his two hundred and ten pounds to their nearest encampment — where he became guest of honor.

But even then his initiation into the ways of the Sioux were not over. He woke up in the night in his tepee, but it was not De Velder's snores that woke him. In front of him stood the Sioux chieftain with a naked dagger which he took care to light up with a torch.

Father De Smet had not much to say. It was the chieftain who spoke : "Black Robe," said he, "are not you afraid ?"

No doubt he was, but he gave the right answer, very expressively, for he took the hand of the Indian, layed it upon his own heart, saying : "See if it beats stronger than usual. — I am as safe in your camp, as in the house of my brother."

At this the Sioux begged him to tell him more about

the Great Spirit. He sent his own son as a guide to Father De Smet. Let the Black Robe instruct him.

At the next Fur Company Fort, Fort Vermillion, he had to give more instructions to the Sioux than either he or they had bargained for. A Sioux war-party arrived with a scalp of the Pottowatomies. Father De Smet had taught the Pottowatomies in Missouri. They had been his charges there, before he had gone to the mountains with the Flat Heads, and he knew that they and the Sioux had made a treaty of peace. Acting now with the prestige of a Black Robe of the French, in the old peace-making manner of Father Marquette and Father Allouez he addressed the Sioux as if he were their own father, and an irate one at that. Such was the effect of his words that they restored peace.

On he went, and on New Year's Eve he was at St. Louis.

Father De Smet's hopes were now soaring higher than they had ever soared in the dreams of his twenties, just as his opinion of the Indians had soared. And in the spring of 1841 — the following spring — he started forth to the same mountains of the Flat Heads, this time to work more permanently. He had with him two other priests, Father Point, who with a very sharp pencil drew pictures of all that he saw, usually with a saint from heaven looking down on the meticulously accurate nature, and Father Mengarini, both Jesuits. And then there were three lay brothers and three other workmen. This time he had his own wagon train for he had raised money for it in New Orleans. And the plan ahead of him was definite and ambitious. He was going to establish a "Christianity" in some fertile valley of the Rockies, in some haunt of the Flat Heads. In it he would teach them to be sedentary. It would be a paradise on a lost horizon.

On Assumption Day he came once again to a meeting with the Flat Heads. This time they had come but three hundred miles to meet him, for he knew the way. Then northward he fared with them, and chose with them and for them a site for their "Christianity." It was on the Bitter Root River (which turns into the Clark), a valley grand in its beauty, and fertile, and near to other friendly tribes. Father De Smet had great hopes for the citadel of the faith which he was founding. It was to be a Paraguay more successful than the famous Jesuit Paraguay of the 17th century. "It seems to us," he wrote to his provincial at St. Louis, "that the little nation of Flat Heads is a chosen people, out of which it is easy to make a model tribe, the kernel of a Christianity not to be exceeded in fervor by that of Paraguay.

"We have," continued the latter, "more resources than had our Spanish Fathers. We can profit by an isolation from the corrupt nations, by an aversion (on the part of the Indians) for the various sects, by a horror of idolatry, by a sympathy for the Whites, especially for the Black Robes, of whom the name to them is synonymous with goodness, wisdom, piety. Furthermore there is to our advantage the central situation of this valley, its emplacement spacious enough for several reductions, a fertile soil, a rampart of high mountains, independence from all authority except that of God and of those who represent Him most immediately ; no tribute to pay except that of prayers ; an appreciation by the Indians already of the advantages of civilized life.   Finally, there is their conviction profoundly held, that without religion one cannot be happy either in this life or the next."

On the feast of Our Lady of Mercy, September 24th, a great cross was erected in the valley of happy promise. The name of the Mission we do not have to ask.   It was St. Mary.

Everything continued to surpass all his expectations, and finally there came a touch of the supernatural which seemed to him to give a Divine approval to his enterprise. It happened on Christmas Eve.   An Indian orphan, Paul, had beheld a strange apparition.   He made no claims for it, himself.   He was a boy without pretense.   He had entered his tepee and had seen — he could not tell which it was a man or woman, for the clothes worn were not such as men or women that he knew wore, but he referred to it as a lady.   "Her feet did not touch the ground ; her robe was white as snow ; she had a star above her head, and under her feet a snake gnawing a fruit that I don't know. From her heart there came forth rays of light which came toward me.   When I saw that, at first I was afraid ; then I wasn't afraid.   My heart was burning, my head clear.   I don't know how it came about, but suddenly I knew my prayers."

What had she said ?   One thing she said.   She was glad that the village of the Flat Heads was called St. Mary.

On the last day of the year Father De Smet wrote a letter of rejoicing to his provincial.   "All the Flat Head nation is converted, and also a few of the Kallispels, the Nez-Percés, the Coeurs-d'Alène, the Snakes, the Kootenay have been baptized ; still other tribes reach out their hands to us. — The whole vast region waits only the arrival of missionaries in order to range itself under the banner of Christ : such, very Reverend Father, is the little bouquet of flowers which we offer you at 1841's end."

Thirty years passed. Thirty-seven years passed. All those years Father De Smet had lived for the "Christianities" of his dream in the Rockies. To accomplish his purpose he had become the world's most tireless traveler. Twice he had gone to those Rockies by sea rounding Cape Horn and going east from Oregon. Six times he ,had gone overland westward from the Missouri. And what traveling he had done in those Rockies and about them, far up into British Columbia ! And what traveling he had done in the United States to collect money, from New Orleans to New York ! And what traveling he had done in Europe on a similar purpose from Rome to Dublin ! There had come a time when so little was being accomplished in comparison with the money raised and the wondrous tales told — for he was a voluminous writer — that even his Jesuit Superior was afraid that he was an over-sanguine man, and at Rome it was whispered that he was the victim of his imagination. Had not his much-vaunted Flat Heads at one moment lapsed ? But Father De Smet's hopes were as high as ever, even higher.

There was but one cause of his unsuccess : the White Man. The traders had done their best to ruin the morals of his mountain tribes. And those who wanted Indian lands had provoked war after war in order to secure it. The Whites had individually no sense of responsibility for them. It was not that they wished to see or cause visible slaughter. But O, that the Indians might disappear! On one occasion they hung up smallpox-infested garments in a tree in order that through natural causes, not through them as human beings, the Indians taking those clothes might die of a plague — nobody guilty. If there was any explicit attitude toward the Indians, among those who had more obligation to be responsible — the statesmen — it was that which De Smet's friend, Thomas H. Benton of Missouri — whose son he had baptized — had made. His statement was at least frank : "The Red Men have disappeared from the shores of the Atlantic : the tribes which tried to stand against them have been exterminated. For my part, I cannot murmur against what seems to be the working of a divine law."

Such an attitude could well discourage Father De Smet, but he always believed that the United States government could and would step in and make some sort of treaty with the Indians which it could and would enforce, even against its own White citizens. It was with this hope that he had twice subdued an Indian revolt by his own prestige and at the request of the United States Army had arranged a peace. Yet every time the peace had been broken and it was the Whites who were the offenders. During the Civil War the Indians had retaliated with a vengeance : the Sioux had seized their opportunity, taken the offensive, and had slaughtered one thousand inoffensive settlers in Minnesota. Now, however, he was once again refounding his hopes, and was in 1868 riding westward with a more distinguished escort than he was used to : five generals of the United States Army, who had won their fame and shown their ability in the Civil War, Sherman, Harney, Sanborn, Terry and Sheridan.

Of these generals Sherman as usual had called a spade a spade. He had declared that there was but one solution : the Sioux would have to be exterminated. War costs money and he stated an enormous figure as necessary for the operation of extermination. But even Sherman was ready to listen to alternatives, and as he rode westward, he had agreed with Father De Smet and the others as to what terms might be offered : a huge reservation north of the River Niobrara in northern Nebraska and extending from the Missouri to the Rockies was to be offered to the Indians as their permanent, inviolable hunting-ground. It was to Father De Smet that the negotiations were to be left. He was acknowledged as the uncrowned monarch of the Indians, and he was given as ambassador from the United States the rank of Major.

One thing was certain : though the peace-making would have to be done piecemeal, it would have to be done with all the tribes and fractions and factions of tribes. Some tribes were ready to make peace, but there was one in particular, that of Sitting Bull on the Powder River, which had declared war to the death. Back in the '50's this tribe had on one occasion *not* joined an Indian uprising but on its approaching an American army-post the officer in command — whose name need not be remembered — had fallen upon it, either fearing treachery, or else obstinate in the assumption that all Indians were alike, and slaughtered it. This outrage the Indians would not forget, nor forgive. To them there was no White Man who did not have a forked tongue.

The first parleying was done at Omaha. There the generals, even General Sherman, were present, and the representatives of many tribes came and submitted to them, but not all. After this it was for Father De Smet to seek out the malcontents. He would go on not so much as a Major in the United States Army as a missionary. He asked the generals to stay behind and then follow later. "A Black Robe," he said, "surrounded by epaulets would seem to hostile Indians very strange, and it would not be very agreeable to them." He would go ahead of the generals up the Missouri and invite the still hostile Indians to meet the generals at Fort Rice.

He went up the Missouri for thirty-two days, to where the Cannon Ball River flows into it. Here was Fort Rice. He found some Indians already there, and won them over to the side of peace. And he baptized some of them, and prepared the Catholic soldiers at Fort Rice to receive Holy Communion on the Day of Pentecost. Then he told the soldiers and the Indians at the Fort that he was going west over the Bad Lands to the Camp of Sitting Bull, to the Indians who had the most resentment against the Whites. On hearing this the Indians at Fort Rice assured him that he was but marching to his sure death : that he could find no better way to lose his scalp.

He assured them that he would not be afraid : he was protected. "Before the picture of the Blessed Virgin, [at St. Louis] Mother and Protectress of all the nations, six lamps were burning for his success day and night."

Some of the Indians expressed themselves as willing to join him. He took with him eighty soldiers, and one trapper who was thoroughly conversant with the language of Sitting Bull. And he rode west.

Nine days passed — not a sign of a Sioux or any other human being. He was nearing Sitting Bull. But it was not well to arrive as a hostile force near to the bands of Sitting Bull. He sent four Indians ahead carrying presents of tobacco, that is, offers of friendship.

Six more days passed — there must have been consultation in the hostile camp — before messengers arrived from Sitting Bull and from his allied chiefs. "Let the Black Robe come. The chiefs are eager to know what he comes for. But let him come alone. If another White Man approaches, he will not return with a whole scalp."

It was on June 19th, 1868, that Father De Smet came in sight of the camp of Sitting Bull at the confluence of the Yellowstone and the Powder Rivers. Four hundred warriors were drawn up as if to make battle against him. Was it not like the case of Father Padilla repeating itself, but this time with a different issue? "Immediately," so Father De Smet tells the story, "I had my standard of peace unfurled, which carried on one side of it the Holy Name of Jesus, and on the other the picture of the Blessed Virgin, surrounded with golden stars. Thinking that they saw the standard of the United States, the Indians halted, and appeared to enter into conversation. The four chiefs galloped towards us, and began to circle around the banner [as they were to circle around and destroy General Custer's command eight years later] but scarcely had they perceived what the banner represented than they gave me their hands, and signalled to their warriors to approach. — I was melted to tears in seeing what reception these sons of the desert, still pagan, prepared for a poor Black Robe."

And peace was made. There came the meeting at Fort Rice, and the Indians were willing to receive and the United States was willing to grant the inviolable, final hunting-grounds.

It was not on a day known so much as a saint's day as a national holiday that Father De Smet started back from Fort Rice toward St. Louis. It was the Fourth of July. I suspect it was the happiest Fourth of July in his life. He had insured — he thought — the salvation of thousands of Indians in this world and in the next : the peace between Indian and White Man had been established, and the missionary work which he had begun could go on without hindrance and with wondrous harvest during his few remaining years of life and after his death. Because of wars he had never been able to Christianize many of the Sioux, but they were ready to be Christianized. Soon he would have a Christian reduction of unparalleled extent. In it would be the sedentary tribes of the Rockies and the buffalo-hunting wanderer, and all would enjoy a single peace, and all would have one sovereign to keep the peace : Our Lady.

Once again he seemed to have been but a blind enthusiast. Within six years gold was to be discovered in the Black Hills and the prospectors entered the reduction as if it had not existed. And what could the United States government do ? Unlike Spain, unlike France, neither the English government nor ours had considered the Indians as really its subjects. The Americans to us at that date, at least, were merely the White Americans, and the

Reds were outsiders ; and the Whites had first to be protected.

But this happened after Father De Smet's death.   He
was not alive to taste this chagrin.   Before his death,
however, something equally disheartening had happened.
President Grant, who as President was more easily misled
than as a general, allowed himself to become responsible
for a solution of the Indian problem, which was dictated
by men who knew nothing of Father De Smet and who
cared less.   The Indians, it was true, were granted missionaries, but many of the missionaries were to be Protestant (which was comprehensible), and some of the
Indian tribes which were Catholics were given to Protestants (which was less comprehensible).   Moreover,
many of the Indian agents who were appointed to the
tribes left to the Catholics were — even contrary to the
law of the solution — not Catholics, but politicians of the
Protestant faith or of no religion.

So Father De Smet's enthusiastic plan, which had
stayed with him youthful to the end, had its failure.   But
as in the case with the Spaniards and with the French the
failure was not total, and it was more apparent than real.
Gradually the injustices to Catholic Indian tribes were
remedied, and from the foundation that Father De Smet
laid even now the harvests are being reaped.   One thing
is certain : he had established over all the Indians of the
Northwest the fame and name of the Mother of God,
to whom he had given the title *Auxillium et Refugium
Indianorum.*

CHAPTER X

SAPIENTIA

IF ONE GOES to the city of Washington now in our time, and then goes out to Brookland — also in the District of Columbia — and comes to the mushroom growth of the Catholic University, its buildings newly-grown and white, rising out of the ground, one sees there among those buildings one which seems from its great size and ponderosity to have sunk back into the ground from which it sprang. It is the crypt of the National Shrine of the Immaculate Conception. It is the foundation of a giant basilica yet to be built. It is a cellar which rises up, not a roof that has sunk in a quicksand. This promise of a future edifice attests to the dedication of our land to Our Lady — all of it, for the shrine to be built is a National Shrine — but it also attests to the dedication of our Catholic system of education to Our Lady, for its site is the grounds of the Catholic University of America which has been planned as a capping to that system, as the keystone in its arch.

Our Catholic University is put under Our Lady's patronage. But if that were all, it would be only what goes without saying. It would not point to any uniqueness in our country or in our university. I am not aware that any university of old Christendom did not take Our Lady for its patron, whether it was the Sorbonne, Prague or Oxford, or, of a later generation, Louvain. This was almost inevitable, for Our Lady personified Divine Sapience. And it was almost necessary to a university's sanity, for without Our Lady's humility the book-learned scholar becomes hideously arrogant, and incurs the loss of his own soul, and the suspicion and then the hatred of the people he looks down upon. The old pontifical universities were all Our Lady's, and all universities which have sprung up since and which may or may not have repudiated the Christian hope, look to her implicitly. They are descended from her universities, their liberty is the liberty she gave, and there is no university which can entirely repudiate the concept of divine wisdom.

The education of Catholics in our country has been identified with Our Lady in a much more unique manner. Of course she watches over it, but also she has performed it, through her images, the sisters, who in our country have had an importance as teachers that they have never had anywhere else in the world. They in an emergency have done both what they were best fitted to do : teach the young of both sexes, but they have also cheerfully done what men (who were lacking) might ideally better do, teach the boys as they near to manhood.

How this came about is a story to set us wondering. Catholics know that the story exists, but they do not often sit down and read it to themselves. Those who are not Catholics do not think it exists. They know full well that there are parochial schools, where black-clothed nuns watch the multi-colored children at play at recess. They may know that a hundred thousand sisters are teaching in these schools. But to them sisters have no history. They come from an inexhaustible supply, manufactured by the Catholic hierarchy as clay images might be made in mass production. They do not ask how they came to be nuns — why should they? — and they do not ask how they happened to be on hand in our American cities for the hierarchy to make use of. The Catholic teaching sisterhoods came into being in our country without those who were thought important in the country even noticing them, and they worked at a work which the historians since have not even bothered to chronicle. This makes their story all the more wonderful, for it was a story of hardship, adventure and success — a very American story; yet unlike kindred stories, it has been kept fresh and unheard.

The first teaching order of nuns to arrive in our country were the Ursulines who came to New Orleans in 1727. No other nuns of any kind had set foot on our territory, not in Spanish Catholic Florida, nor in long-lasting Spanish New Mexico. Their head was Sister Mary Tranchepain of St. Augustine, a convert from Protestantism, and a native of Rouen. With her were nine others. The year 1727 is not an early date in our colonial history, but it was an early date in the history of Louisiana, and the adventures of these arriving sisters belonged to the days when it was somewhat epical for anyone to cross the ocean. Their port of departure was L'Orient, and they were still within sight of that port when their ship became impaled on a rock, which made the captain think they were too holy and brought him bad luck, and should be thrown overboard. Then the ship, freed from the rock, was chased by corsairs. Then the tempests drove them from their course, and then the captain began to wander of his own wish, bent on profitable trading here and there — Caribbean-cruising.

Once again this wandering captain brought his ship to a dead stop on a rock, this time in the Florida waters. Once again he scowled at the sisters and ordered them to throw their trunks into the water. But the scowl this time was but a mask. They had won his respect and chivalry, and to his cost he jettisoned sixty barrels of brandy and numerous bales of sugar, but let them keep their trunks. So they arrived at the Mississippi mouth in a very much lightened ship, and went up the Mississippi in dug-outs, camping out each night. On two of the nights, so they recounted in hilarity, the mattresses on which they slept began to float off with them in their sleep, so wet was the mud in which they lay. And each night they were ordered to land an hour before sunset, so that they could stretch a mosquito netting over their beds. At last New Orleans! How glad they were to see it! They would have been glad to see any city. Sister Stanislas wrote home about it. "The city is very beautiful, but it has not all the beauty the songs attribute to it."

What is a Catholic teaching sisterhood? Let us read some of the paragraphs of the constitution of this particular one of them which was the first to arrive and which began among us their history. "The Ursuline Order has been instituted not only for the salvation and perfection of its members, but also in order that these may help and serve their neighbor by the instruction of young girls, whom they must labor to bring up in the fear and love of God, leading them in the way of salvation, teaching them every social and Christian virtue, and preparing them to be a source of edification to others by the practice of these virtues.

"This vocation is eminent, and it ought to be esteemed by those whom God has called thereto ; for in following it they are doing with advantage the office of the Guardian Angels, an angel being charged to guard a single soul, and that by ways secret and invisible ; whereas an Ursuline can direct several souls by ways exterior, sensible, and proportionate to their capacity. And this need not astonish us, as God has, since the Incarnation of His Divine Son, raised men above angels, to aid and cooperate in the works of Grace."

For forty years during the period of French domination the Ursulines continued to be the "Guardian Angels" of the young girls in New Orleans. It was a city that very much needed visible guardian angels, for the population was composed of two classes, neither of which had very good eyes for anything invisible. One class was that of the lower strata of the population who were largely criminals and outcasts sent from France, and the other was that of the propertied men who were afflicted with a Voltairian skepticism. The Ursuline convent was the Christian citadel of New Orleans. And it did not fall.

Then came the Spanish period of another forty years, and then, in 1804, Louisiana became part of the United States. There fell a fear into the heart of the Mother Superior as to what might be their fate under this still somewhat unknown republic, and she wrote a letter to President Jefferson. President Jefferson knew a good deal about convent schools, for his daughter had attended one near Paris and had desired to become a Catholic and had caused her father to make a very sudden journey in horse and carriage to rescue her. He wrote to the Mother Superior a very reassuring reply :

The President of the United States to Sœur Thérèse de St. Xavier Farjon, Supérieure, and the Nuns, etc. :

I have received, Holy Sisters, the letters you have written to me, wherein you express anxiety for the property vested in your institution by the former Government of Louisiana. The principles of the Government and Constitution of the United States are a sure guarantee to you that it will be preserved to you sacred and inviolate, and that your institution will be permitted to govern itself according to its own voluntary rules, without interference from the civil authority. Whatever diversity of shade may appear in the religious opinions of our fellow-citizens, the charitable objects of your institution can not be indifferent to any ; and its furtherance of the wholesome purposes of society by training up its young members in the way they should go, can not fail to insure it the patronage of the Government it is under. Be assured it will meet with all the protection my office can give it.

I salute you, Holy Sisters, with friendship and respect.

THOMAS JEFFERSON

For more than half a century after the Ursulines arrived in our land there were no other teaching sisters or any religious sisters in it. There was no need for them in uninhabited Louisiana, and on the very much inhabited Atlantic Coast they were not to be tolerated. Except in Pennsylvania no Catholic schools of any kind were allowed to exist. And except in Pennsylvania openly, and in Maryland surreptitiously, they did not exist. In these two provinces the instruction was carried on by men, and what education was given was extraordinarily good. In Pennsylvania the educators were both priests and laymen, and they were Germans teaching the German Catholics. The priests were German Jesuits, but they were more than so many Jesuits who in emergency turned from parish work to teaching. They were learned enough to have filled university chairs in Europe. Father Schneider, who founded a school at Goshenhoppen and there taught children to read and write and to add, was the most learned elementary schoolmaster in English North America : he had been rector of Heidelberg University. As for the teaching laymen, the German Catholics found them for themselves and one account proves that at least one of them was of very good quality. In 1741, an Anglican pastor from Chester, Pennsylvania, wrote in indignation to the Society for the Propagation of the Gospel at London. He complained of the Quakers who sent their children to "a rigid, virulent Papist — in the said town of Chester, in order to oppose and impoverish a Protestant teacher." I doubt very much if the Quakers sent their children to the Papist simply through spite. I suspect that it was because he taught them better than the Protestant.

In Maryland, too, there were laymen and priests who taught Catholic school. Had the Catholics been able to maintain their original rights there, a thorough system of Catholic instruction might here have been established. The *Ark* and the *Dove* had brought over to Maryland a very learned man, Father White, who had once been Professor of Dogmatic Theology and of Hebrew at Valladolid in Spain ; and he and the Jesuits with him laid plans in the 1630's for a Jesuit college in the colony. The Catholic settlers, too, showed an interest in education : in 1653 a certain Edward Cotton of Newtown, Maryland bequeathed his "male and female cattle" and "their increase forever" toward the endowment of a school at Newtown. The Puritan ascendency and the consequent persecution put an end to the grand hopes of the Jesuits, and also to Cotton's endowed Newtown. Yet surreptitiously Catholic education went on, and it was of a high order. Its instructors were Jesuits and they had a school tucked away on the Maryland east shore, near to friendly Pennsylvania, called Bohemia Manor, where enough Marylanders could receive a college-preparation instruction to supply Maryland with a few Catholic leaders in the hour of its need and opportunity, the Revolution. Charles Carroll studied there. And so did his cousin, the future Archbishop. "Jackie Carroll went this day to Marlborough," is a note in the school's old log.

After the Revolution all this changed. Catholics were free to have their own schools. And schools of all kinds were so obviously necessary in a republic where all of a sudden almost everybody was being allowed to vote, that the aid of Catholics was welcomed. Father Molyneux was appointed one of the trustees of the University of Pennsylvania, and Father Richard of Detroit was the first vice-president of the institution which would become the University of Michigan. Bishop Carroll was elected one of the trustees of the Anglican foundation, St. John's College, Annapolis.

There were practically no Catholic laymen fitted to teach school, but such priests as there were, gave a good deal of time to teaching. Georgetown College was founded in 1788 in the District of Columbia by priests who had once been Jesuits and who would become so again when the order was revived. Also the Sulpicians, who had crossed the ocean primarily to train priests, set up in Baltimore a college, St. Mary's, which educated not future seminarians, but future laymen, and laymen of every creed. Likewise the English Dominicans from Flanders taught school in Kentucky, and utterly strange — and witness to the strangeness of the times — the Trappists, Frenchmen, also in Kentucky, took a hand at teaching at Pottinger's Creek for three years. Even bishops became teachers : Bishop England of Charleston was almost the entire faculty of his Philosophical and Classical Institute.

It is possible to laugh at these first Catholic schools and colleges when one hears of their rude buildings and insufficient staff of teachers. But they were not laughed at in their day even by Protestants. These Catholic priests represented not only the Catholic Church but a European humanism which Calvinistic America had been suspicious of. The children of the old colonists, having awakened to a new order of things, wanted to acquire a more cosmopolitan culture and they were ready to go to priests for it. Bishop England of Charleston may have been almost the only teacher in his institute and he may have had to transform himself from a mathematician into a classicist by going out through a schoolroom door and coming back through it with a changed grimace, yet he attracted in Charleston two hundred pupils, and two-thirds of them were Protestants.

It was not that the schools were inadequate in quality : Father Brosius, renowned mathematician from the Rhineland, was not inadequate to teaching short division at Conewago in Pennsylvania.   But numerically they were inadequate, and they had to remain inadequate so long as there was a shortage of Catholic laymen or Catholic priests to teach : and there was no probability that the shortage would cease.   American vocations were very few, and Europe was beginning to have a shortage of priests.   Far from sending over more priests, France under Napoleon began to recall her priests.   And even Ireland lacked priests, for many of the Irish candidates for the priesthood had been accustomed to receive their training on the Continent, and on the Continent during the period of the French Revolution there had been nowhere to train, and they had to wait for their own Maynooth.

Therefore the priests took to enlisting the help of pious women.   This could happen only where there were pious women, where there was something of a settled Catholic community.   In Baltimore a Frenchman, Father Moranville, established a school for the poor. The poor were so many that he could not, like Bishop England, teach them all : he had to have help.   The women of Baltimore were enlisted.   Father Nerinckx did the same in Kentucky.   Father Leonard Neale did the same at Washington, D.C., and Father Richard did the same at Detroit.   At Detroit he did it so thoroughly that he established a complete municipal system of education.   He could do this because Detroit was at this time

an almost completely Catholic town, and he was its acknowledged leader, so much so that he was elected to
Congress and remains the one Catholic priest in our
country to have been so honored.   Our modern systems
of municipal education are not derived from Father Richard's experiment, but they bear a resemblance to his.
He and his pious ladies solved many problems in a way in
which they were to be solved later.

These pious ladies not only took the place of nuns, not
only in many instances lived like nuns, but they became
nuns.   Out of these groups of teachers came several
Catholic orders which sprang to life on our soil : the
American version of the Sisters of Charity of the foundation of Mother Seton ; the Visitation Sisters at Washington ; the Sisters of Loretto and the Sisters of Nazareth,
both completely American, and both of Kentucky ; and
the Sisters of the Blessed Virgin of Philadelphia, who
were driven from Philadelphia in the riots of the '40's
to Dubuque.   Thus the need of teachers was the origin
of many of our indigenous religious orders of women,
even though those orders after their foundation were interested in more than merely teaching.

Also to help the few Catholic men teachers came
teaching orders of women from across the water.   In
1818, Mother Duchesne of the Society of the Sacred
Heart, with four others of her order, sailed from Bor-
deaux, France, to New Orleans in a ship called the *Re-
becca.*   Mother Duchesne in the zeal of her heart had
since childhood daily said a prayer of St. Francis Xavier
for more missionaries.   She had always herself wished to
be a missionary.   Now at the age of fifty she was becom-

ing one. She came from traditionalistic France. She brought the Old World with her. She brought the past with her : her superior Saint Sophie Barat had presented her at her departure with a silver statue of Our Lady of the Pillar of Saragossa. So Our Lady of the Spaniards took her to the mouth of the river which the Spaniards had called the River of the Holy Spirit three hundred years before, and took her up that river past the burial place of De Soto ; Our Lady of the Pillar took her through the memories of the past, but amid the new circumstances, and by the newest means of locomotion : a steamboat. She came to the Missouri River and there she disembarked and founded an academy, from which there grew before her death three other academies in the Mississippi Valley.

Mother Duchesne was fifty when she arrived in our country, but what suppleness of spirit she had ! She had never particularly wanted to come to an American frontier town, like St. Charles or Florissant, or St. Louis. St. Louis at that time was undergoing a real estate boom, and it was impossible for her community to buy in it land at any possible price. It was not at a place like St. Louis that she had conceived of herself as a missionary. She had wished to be a missionary to the Chinese, or, second best, to the American Indians. Yet to the boom days of the Mississippi she acclimated herself. She lived on till she was eighty-one, till she had been for thirty-one years an American. Just before she died she left a bit of advice to those of her order, which has been followed by her order and by all orders which have come so generously from Europe to us. "Renounce lawful satisfaction, adapt yourself to characters of different nationalities, see God always in His creatures, and live with them as children of one Father."

Mother Duchesne in her day went to a far frontier, for St. Louis was a far frontier from her home at Grenoble, France, but another community of nuns went even farther, and, though it was somewhat later, to a frontier which was even more an early frontier. These were the Sisters of Notre Dame de Namur. They took a seven months' voyage with Father De Smet from Antwerp to Oregon in 1843, round Cape Horn. Father De Smet needed them to teach at the mouth of the Columbia River, and he did not think that it was well to have them pass by the Oregon Trail. He preferred for them, though not for himself, the all-sea route.

No doubt he was right, but he did not lead them to escape all dangers and all difficulties. Far from it. Some of the hardships were due to the constant caprice of nature. Contrary winds delayed them a month at the very harbor mouth. Rounding the Horn they were attacked by a Cape Horn storm which drove them toward the Patagonian shore. All seemed lost and Father De Smet visited the nuns as they crouched in the dark under hatches — six of them. Did they want to confess ? No, they were quite tranquil. And the wind changed. And on they went.

Other hardships had a more human cause. "No sooner," writes Father De Smet, "had we put out to sea than we experienced the bad management of the provider. An odor of decomposition pervaded the vessel. To his annoyance the captain was obliged to order the meat to be thrown overboard." Then the living fowls died, before they could be eaten. If only the rats would die likewise ! Or rather, if only they would die by leaping overboard ! There were so many rats that they had that rat-arrogance of running over people, even people awake. At Valparaiso a rat census and a rat-massacre was made. Fourteen hundred rats !

Finally after the due months and the due storms the ship came to the Columbia River. Here the Captain erred. He tried to pilot his ship, which had carried nobly its title *L'Infatigable*, into the river, but he blundered and took the south entrance to the river, which was all shoals and bars and could not be used, and which was not used. When he was on the boiling of the shoals and when his line told him that every instant the shoals were shoaling, he was aware that something was wrong. — Six fathoms. — Five fathoms. — Three fathoms. — Two and a half. This was the end of all. The keel was on the shoal. — Three fathoms. — The ships had taken the wrong entrance. All was lost. But now the ship bounded on from shoal to shoal, as if it were becoming a land animal, on into deeper water, on into safety. It had taken the wrong entrance, but had established a record of taking it rightly. And it was a good day to take it rightly : it was St. Ignatius Day, July 31st. Weeks back the nuns and the Jesuits had dedicated the ship to the Very Holy and Immaculate Heart of Mary. At any rate it most unconcernedly came to anchor.

By the year 1840, there were fourteen Catholic orders of women teaching in the United States, eight of whom had come to us by direct transplantation from Europe.

There were at that date two hundred parish schools in our country and most of them were conducted by these women. Yet up to 1840 these orders had not been so conspicuous for creating parish public schools as for creating academies, or schools for those who had at least a little money. The word academy has a classical sound, but the founder of the first American Academy, in 1751, in Philadelphia, was Benjamin Franklin, who was too utilitarian to show in it much respect for a classical education. For a hundred years academies flourished in the United States. There were six thousand of them in 1850, and their pupils numbered over a quarter of a million. Their variety lent a charm to them and was probably fruitful of progress. In the main in spite of Franklin's influence they turned their back on utilitarianism and clung in the case of schools for boys to Latin and even Greek. Among these six thousand academies the Catholic academies for girls had considerable repute. In the Mississippi Valley they were the schools of fashion even for Protestants. The Catholic sisters taught a graciousness of manner, and added an amenity to life, which persuaded families that wanted their daughters to be ladylike to send these daughters to them. But not only was this true in the Mississippi Valley ; even on the seaboard it was true. In 1826 for instance a bequest from Father John Thayer had enabled some Ursulines from Canada to establish an academy in the Puritan citadel, Boston, at Mt. St. Benedict, Charlestown. The academy had no long life, for it was burned down by a mob incited by Lyman Beecher and whiskey in 1834, but during its life it was frequented more by Protestants than Catholics, since it taught French and painting and music for the polite education of young girls, and the Catholics who could afford such accomplishments were few. Up to 1840, then, it seemed as if the teaching sisters would be largely associated with academies.

But about 1840 they were called to a different destiny, for the circumstances completely changed. The change was caused partly by the influx of hordes of immigrants, and also by a change in the national customs of education. Up to 1840 it had been taken for granted that all education was religious education. The fear of God was the beginning of wisdom. All schools therefore were religious schools, and denominational. Since there were numerous denominations, not all of them on good speaking terms with their neighbors, and since the various Protestant clergymen who had their little schools were often quite satisfied with their own methods — good and bad — and did not want to learn from the neighboring minister, this system — it must be acknowledged — was not a system at all. Its inefficiency, its inability to develop, led to the arising of a movement of school-reform, at the head of which was Horace Mann. He wished to change and exchange the time-honored American method for a Prussian method of state schools, in which there would be coordination and centralization, in which, in short, denominationalism would have to disappear, and the ministers would have to resign their profession as schoolmaster. He was not totally irreligious, but since religion, as it was, interfered with school efficiency, let religion be taken out of the schools.

Horace Mann met his first opposition not from Cath-

olics, but from Protestant ministers.   They had no wish
to abdicate ; and their people were generally behind
them.   If they had continued in their opposition they
might have at least arranged a compromise whereby religious teaching might have been retained at no very
great cost to their authority.   There would have continued to be denominational schools, supervised by various state and city authorities, living by subsidies from
taxes levied by those authorities.   The country was religious enough and conservative enough to have preferred
this.

But the Protestant ministers ceased their opposition because of their inability to swallow the distasteful pill of
having Catholic schools likewise subsidized.   They were
ready to receive the Prussian system rather than have the
Catholics so favored.

It was in New York State that this change of front
occurred.   In that State there had been until 1824 Catholic schools receiving government subsidies.   The subsidies were not as much as the Catholics numerically deserved, but the Catholics were people content not to have
all they merited.

Other religious bodies also received aid for their
schools.   Among them was a body, professedly non-
denominational but which was merely negatively Protestant, that is, anti-Catholic.   This body was the Public
School Society.   In 1824 somehow or other this body
had been by the State Legislature made extraordinarily
prominent.   The Legislature had empowered the Common Council of the City of New York to name the or-
ganizations to which City educational aid should go.

The Common Council allotted all the educational subsidies to the Public School Society, with the exception of some small portions to various orphan asylums. This made the Public School Society supreme, and in its supremacy it conducted schools in which the Catholic Church was constantly attacked, in which no Catholic could feel at home.

While the Catholics were being deprived of any subsidies and were, out of their own poverty, taxing themselves for their own schools in which there were three thousand pupils, there came to the see of New York a very courageous, even pugnacious bishop, Bishop Hughes. Although he was a man not to be deterred by any difficulties, he let this unjust treatment continue. Even though there was something insidious and tricky about the Public School Society which would have aroused any honest man's ire he remained though still honest yet calm. The children of his people were receiving no education or mis-education, and it pierced his heart to see their lot, yet he held his tongue. And even though there seemed to be no possibility that his people could ever with their pennies build a school system of their own, he continued to face the future, not calculating all its perils, finding it too desolating so to calculate. Indeed, he might not have made any move at all if there had not been Protestants who resented the Public School Society receiving all the funds, and who wished to have money given once again to their denominational schools. President Nott of Union College, a Protestant, urged him to make a move, and so did the Scotch Presbyterians, to whom the wishy-washy Protestantism taught by the Public School

Society's schools was nauseating, and so did the Hebrew Congregation of New York. Also he had the support of the State's Governor, William H. Seward, who had addressed a message to the Assembly at Albany: "The children of foreigners, found in great numbers in our populous cities and towns, and in the vicinity of our public works, are too often deprived of the advantages of our system of public education, in consequence of prejudices arising from difference of language and religion. It ought never to be forgotten that the public welfare is as deeply concerned in their education as in that of our children. I do not hesitate, therefore, to recommend the establishment of schools in which they may be instructed by teachers speaking the same language with themselves, and professing the same faith."

Bishop Hughes then sent a petition to the Common Council of the City asking that money be allotted to Catholic and Protestant schools, as well as to the pet schools of the Public School Society. He wished to conciliate the reformers who followed Horace Mann. He saw that there was truth in what they said about educational inefficiency. Let the State, if it wished to, be allowed to examine the teachers in Catholic schools, and demand of them a certain grade, let it be allowed to inspect the manner and matter of instruction. Let it even forbid the teaching of Catholic dogmas. All the Catholics asked was one thing: that their schoolbooks should not preach against the Church.

This might seem to us an unwise surrender, even though made by a man known never to surrender unless the surrender were more than wise. But it was not received by some Protestant fanatics as a surrender at all, but rather as a Papal challenge, and in the clamor that they raised the surrender was not accepted. Only one member of the City's Common Council dared to vote to accept it; the others were cowed by a fury which they realized it was political death to oppose : the old Colonial anti-Catholic phobia. The State Legislature at Albany, being at a distance from the heated oratory that went on in New York, was able more than the Common Council to keep its head. It came to the conclusion, however, that religion was such a cause of conflict and high feeling that it was well to have done with it in the schools. It put the educational funds in charge of a State board, who would establish State schools, completely the State's. No private body, not even the Public School Society, would receive even a cent. Thus a few Protestant agitators by their ineptitude handed over the victory in New York State to Horace Mann and led to the nationwide acceptance of a foreign experiment : the State school system of State-worshipping Prussia.

From that time on Catholics realized that in order to have schools where religion was taught, they would have to build them themselves and support them themselves. In short, they would have to have a Horace Mann system of their own with religion maintained in it.

Then and there began a Catholic enterprise which is more than anything else a matter of pride to the Catholic of the United States. "The greatest religious fact in the United States today," said Bishop Spalding a half century ago, "is the Catholic school system, maintained without any aid except for the people who love it."

In 1840 there were two hundred parish schools, elementary and secondary, in the United States. A little less than a hundred years later there were forty times as many — there were over 9,000. And the schools themselves were larger : there were in them three million pupils, well over a half of those who were theoretically to be taken care of. A half success but even then what an incredible success !

And it is the sisters who have made this success possible. Just how many there are at any moment engaged in teaching no one exactly knows : ninety thousand it is estimated, eight times as many as the men engaged in Catholic teaching. They belong to ten times eight orders, some of whose names are widely familiar, others that are known only where they work. Some of those who have most lately arrived come from orders which give awe by their ancientry. "Arrived," we read, "in the United States 1911, founded in Cappadocia the fourth century, the Sisters of St. Basil," six hundred and six of them. St. Basil and the United States ! And there are sisters of the Ruthenian rite, and Sisters from Lithuania of St. Casimir, and Missionary Sisters of the Sacred Heart founded by Saint Francis Xavier Cabrini while some of us were already alive, and Sisters of St. Mary of the Presentation who came in 1903 to Wild Rice, North Dakota, and Sisters of Notre Dame de Sion, identified with the conversion of the Jews, who came to Kansas City in 1912. If any one wants to discover that our country is more than a greatly expanded New England village, or than an Earl of Warwick stock company, he has only to read a list of these sisterhoods. What seeds there are in this country yet to spring up, if we do not make our land a land of stones !

And how did these sisters arrive ? Was it that the bishops whistled for them ? In 1838, Bishop Bruté of Chicago dreamed of having sisters for his schools, but he had ended by laughing at himself : "I dream of Sisters ! But how so ?" And twelve years later Bishop Kenrick of Philadelphia had decided not to dream even of having sisters, or any kind of teachers. "I am fully sensible of the importance of Catholic schools, but I do not know how we are to establish them. Teachers of a religious character are not easily had, and schoolhouses are wanting."

Europe's misfortune sent some of them. Germany persecuted sisters into exile during the Kulturkampf. France in the days of Combes did likewise. Some countries sent such a large immigration to us that with the fraction of the nation that arrived came also the religious communities that belonged to it. Other countries overflowed with vocations, and their zeal was not happy except when it was founding new religious orders. Old France, except in its off moments, was this way, and New France, Canada, was more so. Some eighteen of the sisterhoods in our midst depend still on central houses in Canada. And where would we be without the orders — men and women — founded in France in the 19th century which have either been driven to us by France's government or thrust to us by God's grace ?

But the story of how they came can also be told in terms of individuals, for an order does not derive its propulsion from the fact that it is an order but from the fact that it is composed of personalities. In the utterly quiet way in which the various sisterhoods came into our country's life, as if they walked silently and on snow and on some dark midnight, it is a relief not to have to find the raucousness of self-assertive personalities such as we find in the building of a railroad, or of cities, or of other human achievements. There is a kind of laughter in our hearts at seeing how without fuss and fury these images of Our Lady accomplished so much when so many others — celebrities, men of force — were accomplishing so little with so much conflict and publicity. Yet it would be a bit blind not here and there to try to discern some woman who with God's help was responsible for great deeds. For there had to be great deeds done in the founding of so many schools. For there was poverty, and poverty, and poverty, the Catholics being everywhere very poor. And there was opposition, and opposition, for the old books against nuns, the pornographic reading of before the Civil War, had done its unending harm.

I choose therefore one nun, one foundress of schools and convents. And I choose an Irish one. And I choose her because she was able, because she worked in so many places and lived so long, and because as Irish she was identified with the one greatest element of Catholic immigration — the Irish immigrants. Her name was Mother Xavier Warde.

Mother Xavier Warde brought over to this country an Irish congregation, the Sisters of Mercy, which had been founded by Catherine McAuley in the early nineteenth century. The sisters of this order were to be less active than the Sisters of Charity, more active than the Carmelites. The name may suggest the work that they chose for themselves. They were to care for the poor, to nurse the sick, and to house the orphans, and also to teach. Even in our country where they were needed so much for teaching, and where they now teach one hundred thousand pupils, they were never to abandon their primary occupation with the poor.

Mother Warde, who brought the congregation, crossed the ocean in the beginning of a new era of travel, in the largest liner then afloat, the *Queen of the West.* It was in 1843, the year when the Sisters of Namur went to Oregon. The ship had sails and steam, yet even then the crossing lasted a month. There were seven in the party ; they traveled by rail from New York to Philadelphia and then took the stage to Pittsburgh — the Fort Duquesne of a hundred years back. Pittsburgh had just been made the seat of a bishop, Bishop O'Connor, a man who had consented to be made bishop only on the condition that when his work was well started he could leave his mitre and join the Jesuits and not be known any longer as a bishop.

At Pittsburgh Mother Warde established a free school and then somehow, against her wishes, one of the Catholic academies which still even in these days of immigration and anti-Catholic fanaticism had their prestige. Her academy was attended by over a hundred pupils, twelve of them Protestant. She had to do everything quickly and she did everything quickly. No sooner was one free school built than it had to be abandoned : it was too small. Her decisions came quick. In 1845 she took

over an orphan asylum.   In 1847 there was typhus ; she
had to establish a hospital.   In 1848, the great year of
Irish immigration, she found her free school had twice
as many pupils as the year before.   At the same time
eight of her sisters died of typhus.

But then as if her difficulties at Pittsburgh were not
enough she established a school at Chicago.   When she
went there in 1846, the city of the old portage had fifteen
thousand inhabitants.   Some of her pupils were Indians.
She thus touched the origin of Chicago, as she touched
that of Pittsburgh.

But she was only beginning her work.   Although she
worked quickly, she had the perseverance of a tortoise.
She established a house in Loretto, Pennsylvania, the
Catholic colony, founded by Prince Gallitzin.   And,
scarcely had she finished that, than she was invited to
Providence, Rhode Island, to the New England where in
the industrial centers like Providence the Catholic population at this time doubled annually, with all the confusion that such an increase involved.

At Providence she had no sooner founded her school
than she was warned by the mayor to leave the city.
Ten thousand Native Americans of the Know-Nothing
Movement were marching on the city to burn her convent.   She had been quick, she had been persevering.
And now she was firm.   She was more of a man than
the mayor.   "If I were Chief Executive," she said, "of
municipal affairs, I would know how to control the
populace."   The mob arrived.   She went into the convent garden where some Irishmen had come with guns
to protect her.   She bade them not to fire unless they

were attacked.   Then she faced the mob.   They hissed.
But the convent was not sacked.   The rioters felt shame
enough to depart.

All this took stamina, but stamina came easily to her,
and she had not exhausted her supply of it.   At Manchester, New Hampshire, she incurred a similar danger
as at Providence.   There she came at the invitation of
a Father McDonald who was a patriarch of the Catholic
workers in that mill-center.   These workers usually
agreed with their pastor, and were certainly not cow-
ardly.   Yet they begged him not to bring the sisters to
Manchester : the feeling against nuns was too strong.
All the Catholics would suffer.   Father McDonald persevered in his intention.   The Sisters of Mercy came,
and very soon all the Catholic children were receiving
their religious education.   She had passed on her courage
to the mill-workers.

But this was not all.   This semi-contemplative woman
had to be able to change plans.   When the Civil War
came she had to turn to staffing various military hospitals
with her sisters, one at Washington, one at Jefferson City.
After the war her adaptability took a new turn.   She
occupied herself with the Catholic Indians of Maine,
founded a school for them in Old Town, amid the Abenakis, and while she was doing that, sent some other sisters to California.   Then she died.   It was in 1879.
There were few public men who were so acquainted
with the diverse provinces of our country and its diverse moods as this immigrant.   And she was but one
of many — the nuns of the great emergency.

The very fact that a century of Catholic children in

our country were educated by nuns gives to our Catholic education a dedication to Our Lady.

Our Lady has a direct connection with the Catholic educational system of our country by standing at the pinnacle of it, like the cross on a church that sparkles in the sunlight and blinds. She affirms, merely by standing there, that there is a Divine Wisdom. But her relation to our country has been even more intimate. She has done more than stand as our pinnacle. She has enabled the poor and the oppressed, and the rich too, to be free from the tyranny of man by being able to have their earthly kind of Divine Wisdom. She has supplied the sisters who, when there was wine but none to serve it, became servers of it, and saved our children, not only our Catholic children, but others indirectly, from becoming puppets. Archbishop Carroll was constant in his petitions to Our Lady — Salve Regina ; so was Father De Smet. So are we. But it is a pleasure also to thank her for the petitions granted. In our way of education what have we not to thank her for. — Thank you for the nuns. —

CHAPTER XI

THE CONTINUANCE

IN THE earliest yesterday of our land Our Lady was sovereign. The Spaniards under Philip II, the French under Louis XIV saw her above them in the sky. She was not as earthly as their earthly sovereigns, but she was just as real, more imperial, and more near — and in moments of peril a thousand times more near. In telling the story of our land's earliest days one can no more leave her out than one could tell about France in the reign of King St. Louis, and leave out that sovereign.

Later on her sovereignty ceased to be acknowledged, save by a humbled minority. It was as if a bright cloud covered her in the sky, which hid her from all as a thin cloud hides the sun and yet is made bright by it. To all except those few who knew her she was unrecognized. Yet what few great things those few liege men of hers did do, they did them in her name, and with constant prayers for her intercession. Some of those great things done by the few have been great not only for those few, but for the nation as a whole. Historians of our country who are thinking only of "1688 and all that" often, though with the best intentions of being fair, find it very hard to weave Catholic history into their history writing. As a rug-maker repudiates some colors, there being no place for them, so they leave out what seems to spoil the unity of their writing. In the history written however in terms of thousands of years it is not so difficult to include the history of Catholic exiles, Catholic immigrants, and even Catholic bishops and Catholic sisters. Such a history shows Our Lady even in the 19th century as rather more important than the Goddess of Liberty who after all is but a bronze, lifeless, dehumanized shadow of her.

But what of the future? Or rather what of the present?

The Puritan descendant of Puritans made a caustic remark concerning his ancestors — which I have already quoted — to the effect that they got rid of Our Lady in order to begin the fight with evil all over again. They were fighters, and the sense of evil gave them a good excuse for a fight. They did begin the fight all over again. They saw Evil everywhere.

Since then the descendants of the Puritans have suffered a great change. It is long since that they gave up viewing all human nature as so fallen that no good be expected of it. By the time of the Revolution it was by some of our leaders — lawyers, and merchants, and Unitarian ministers — being looked on as utterly good and needing only to be left alone. This complete confidence in human goodness — with all the impossible contradictions it involves — has become the religion of Puritans of today, as Calvinism was the religion of Puritans yesterday. There has been a complete theological change in the religion of Protestants in the United States. Once to them the Catholics were too lax. Now the Catholics are too austere.

Yet it would be hard to say that the new attitude has

brought these newer Puritans any nearer to the Delight of Christians. They have turned towards humanism and joyousness, and have found pleasures, but have not been joyous. They talk about delight but except in a literary make-believe they have never found any delight. A century back there came in New England what some have called a Renaissance and others a "Flowering." There was an earnest attempt shown to be human and gay by some poets. There was also an attempt very ministerial and oracular to become profound and philosophical. But there was no "flowering," for a flowering suggests delight, and delight there was not. Santayana, cat-like, pouncing on his victim, was more accurate when he termed what happened "a harvest of leaves." Remote, unvisited pagans in Borneo, for all I know, may, if they have never been Christian, gain a certain delight out of their worship of strange gods. It is a simple delight and the best they can have ; it is worship. But to a Christian, to one whose ancestors were Christian, and who continues even vaguely in the manners his ancestors had and in their way of speech, there is but one delight that can fill his whole being, that is not a mere means of momentary escape, an inebriation, a pleasure — and that is Our Lady. The Puritans in going from their old theology to their new have simply passed Our Lady by, as if she had nothing to do with their first position, their last position, and the change between the two.

There are exceptions, however ; there is Henry Adams himself. He at least realized that Our Lady had everything to do with the first ferocity of these Puritans and then of their change in mood and their last ferocity. He

saw European history and American history in terms of
Our Lady with a discernment which speaks well for the
steadiness of his gaze, and for the courage of his intellect
which was ready to grasp truths that were unwelcome
and thorny. He saw but two alternatives for himself
and for civilization : either to be loyal or disloyal to her.
Whatever decision he may have made in regard to this
in his own heart, his sympathies in his most intimate writings — his poems, his only two poems — incline to loyalty
to her.

The first of these poems is the "Prayer to the Virgin of
Chartres." In it he sings of himself as if he were seven
hundred years old, and seven hundred years wise :

> When your Byzantine portal was still young
> I prayed there with my master Abailard ;
> When Ave Maris Stella was first sung,
> I helped to sing it here with Saint Bernard.

Then the years passed. He pursued a search for truth,
and he turned his back on Our Lady in what he considered to be a well-meaning quest :

> I thought the fault was yours that foiled my search ;
> I turned and broke your image on its throne,
> Cast down my idol, and resumed my march
> To claim the father's empire for my own.

> Crossing the hostile sea, our greedy bànd
> Saw rising hills and forests in the blue ;
> Our father's kingdom in the promised land !
> — We seized it, and dethroned the father too.

And now we are the Father, with our brood,
Ruling the Infinite, not three but One ;
We made our world and saw that it was good ;
Ourselves we worship, and we have no Son.

Such was Henry Adams's summary of the story of the Puritans. The poem sounds as if he thought they had taken a wrong road. The wrong road had led him to where it was impossible to turn back to the old days, but to where another cross-roads opened ahead. One road led to Our Lady and to the reverence for personality, to Christian happiness, the other led to a repudiation of all supernatural religion, to a jettisoning of not only already jettisoned Calvinism, but of the liberal Christianity which had succeeded Calvinism ; it led — he saw it clearly — to the acceptance of the dynamo as god, and to the worship of blind power.

He recoiled as Charles Péguy had recoiled in a similar dilemma, and the poem which he wrote, *Prayer to the Dynamo*, is strangely reminiscent of some of Péguy's rhythms (which I am not aware that he had even heard of) :

Help me to see ! not with my mimic sight —
With yours ! which carried radiance, like the sun,
Giving the rays you saw with — light in light —
Tying all suns and stars and worlds in ours.

Help me to know ! not with my mocking art —
With you, who knew yourself unbound by laws ;
Gave God your strength, your life, your sight, your heart,
And took from him the Thought That Is — The Cause.

But Henry Adams remains alone. He has had numerous Puritan readers, but few Puritan followers. So far as I know, very few of them have ever taken his talk about Our Lady as anything more than "literature." There have been, of course, numerous Puritans who have become Catholics, and who have through baptism and its graces returned to an understanding of Our Lady's place, but they came as individuals, and their point of departure was not his point of departure. He is descended from Puritans and thinks by and for them, yet he does not represent them. There is no visible indication that the Puritans are with one mind — the mind of Henry Adams — returning to sing Salve Regina with Saint Bernard.

But what of the Catholics? They do not compare with the Puritans in number. They are but one-fifth of our country's population, though they are twenty times as large a proportion of our population as in Archbishop Carroll's time. What of them?

Of course no Catholic can *not* honor Our Lady ; it is logically and psychologically impossible *not* so to do. But do these one-fifth of the population continue to weave Our Lady into this country's history as intimately as it was of old? Does it continue to be a Marial enterprise? Or has the *Santa Maria's* furrow closed up? Or are Bishop Carroll's prayers at Loretto Shrine a thing of the past? Have these Catholics outgrown, as it were, the necessity of her special protection? Our Lady is nothing in comparison with the Holy Trinity. Perhaps we are so holy that we do not need so much help from her as before in order to approach the Holy Trinity. Perhaps we are so stainless ourselves that we do not have to turn to her to rejoice in human nature.   Perhaps many things.

We cannot really answer these questions.   It would take a congress of guardian angels to give much evidence on the matter.   But we can make some easy observations which we do not often make, not because they are difficult, but because we so seldom give ourselves time for anything so simple.   The first of these observations is that Catholics have escaped the crossroads that faced Henry Adams.   They are incapable of hesitating as to whether they would choose a dynamo or a personality. It seems laughable to balance the two — "Which do you like best, Peter Smith or Peter Smith's cane ?" — A dynamo is something for a personality to use, not be used by. A dynamo, no matter how large, can at best be a toy to present to Our Lady.   And in order that it be appropriately presented, let it be blessed.   There is in the Church's prayerbook a proper blessing for a dynamo, for a machine to make electricity.   It is listed quite congruously next to the blessing for myrrh — machine and myrrh both beginning with *m* :

O Lord God, all powerful, Who art founder of every light, bless this machine newly founded for the awakening of light : and be with us, in order that to Thee Who art the light that never fails, we after the murkiness of this world may have power to come.

There is no danger of a machine's eclipsing Our Lady.
And then there is another even more self-evident observation to make.   Catholics have not grown so highbrow that they are in any danger of replacing her — a

human being — by an abstract ideal. The matter does not even have to be discussed. Wait till we are philosophers and have the maladies of philosophers.

All this is negative. It proves that she is in no danger of being eclipsed — nothing more. To make a more positive observation is, however, delicate : it might sound like boasting. Let us have the enemies of the Catholic faith speak for us. Let us hear them say, as they do, that American Catholics continue to be those superstitious people who carry "beads" in their pockets. But that is to be expected ; that has gone on for a long time. For Catholics to say prayers to the Blessed Virgin is not incongruous, since the prayers are Catholic prayers, and the Catholics have a right to do with Catholic things as they want. But worse than that, they have of late in their cockiness been taking perfectly good American activities and offering them to her as if they did not belong to the United States. Consider football, for instance. That is an American invention and up-to-date. Yet the Catholic University of Notre Dame, to go no further, plays football for Our Lady, tackles, punts, makes touchdowns for Our Lady — for Notre Dame. Don't they know that the very name of Notre Dame should be associated with such things as Chartres Cathedral and with artists who look at windows that are more beautiful than jewels ? Notre Dame is medieval, football is modern. It is bad taste that confuses them. What are the Catholics trying to do, medievalize America ?

The truth is we cling to Our Lady in our very special American need. Some of the moral ideas about us are pagan. — But leave that out. — We live at least in a country not superficially spiritual.   There are not — not for many of us — beautiful cathedrals before our faces.   The angelus does not ring.   The hills and valleys are not rich and mysterious with holy legend as in Europe.   We are in exile.   Yet we need, as all men do, something of Heaven.   And we rely on her in our dearth to be among us, to act as Our Queen — beautiful and beautifying — and make our landscape at one stroke heavenly.

We dare call her among us, moreover, because her coming introduces among us nothing foreign, and our reception of her faces her with nothing unfamiliar.   Catholics in the United States need her to establish them in their own American citizenship.   Only in her can they find the means of perpetuating certain qualities which have been called American and which are in danger of disappearing.

We live in a land of hopefulness — hopefulness founded till recently on a belief that everything must get better and better.   Catholics to be true Americans need that hopefulness, but they cannot found it on any such superstition of progress.   They have to turn to Our Lady for it.

We are a land trusting in the goodness of human nature — our human nature. — Catholics have no such luck to see that goodness in themselves.   They have to look to Our Lady for it, and so looking they can really rejoice.

But if our country simply stayed at home and said "Our Lady does all for us, we are her country," then we should soon cease to be hers.   She may so love our country that she Americanizes us.   But she used our land as a stepping-stone as she does all lands.   She was interested

in us as an addition to Christendom, and she is interested
in us now as a country which continues to add to Christendom. — One does not need to have been raised to a
third Heaven to know this. — Our country, to put it very
soberly, in order to remain hers had to send out the missionaries which our land had received.

Up to the year 1908 we were, in the eyes of the Successor of Saint Peter (who has a long memory and who measures time not quite as we who build a sky-scraper in a
few weeks and stay awake nights thinking how we can
do it quicker), a missionary country.   On the books we
were still the country to which missionaries came, as came
the Franciscans to California, carrying Our Lady's picture as a banner.   After 1908, however, we were considered of age to carry the banner ourselves.   We could
be our own Junípero Serra to others.   But were we?

In 1840, as early as that, the Holy Father had asked the
young church in the United States to go forth, missionary.   Liberia was chosen as the place it should work, and
the choice was appropriate.   Liberia was a portion of
Africa to which it was hoped some of our American negroes who had been stolen and brought here as slaves,
could return as to a homeland.   We had put an end to
the slave-trade soon after our independence from England, but we had inherited the institution of negro
slavery, and we had a special debt to the negroes.   At
the sixth provincial council of Baltimore, which dedicated
our land to the Immaculate Conception, several of the
bishops who should have been there were not there.
Bishop Blanchet of Oregon was too busy to have a year
to spare in order to make the voyage back and forth from

the Columbia River to Baltimore. Also a Bishop Barron, Irish by birth, was absent. He had gone to Liberia to be bishop.

But Bishop Barron did not stay in Africa. Even toward the end of the century when our country was becoming in the eyes of our neighbors all too imperialistic, and was surely a bit meddlesome in wanting to spread our own special civic ideals over the whole world, our Church was a stay-at-home Church. Except for a few individuals who joined foreign orders, we had no missions. It was a matter of regret, it began to be a matter of shame. Nor could our failure be caused by pointing to the need of priests in our own country. That excuse even in the days of Our Lord began to be not an excuse.

Shortly before the Spanish War during which we ousted Spain from Cuba, Puerto Rico and the Philippines, we began to show feeble signs that we were ready to carry on a work which Spain in past centuries had to our profit performed. It was in the year 1896 that the Society for the Propagation of the Faith was founded in this country. This meant that our money at least was to flow toward foreign missions. In 1822 this Society had had its original and French foundation, and during three-quarters of a century it had been sending us money that amounted to at least six million dollars. With our churches and schools to build and the moneyed class being not ours, we had needed the money badly. But by 1896 Catholics were beginning to share in the wealth of this country of wealth, and the debt began to be repaid. Within fifteen years after 1896 we had given back to the Society twice what it had given us.

But this was nothing. It was the sending forth of men that was important, not the paying for others to be sent forth. And that, too, at about the time of the War with Spain began to begin. Since 1896 we have become a country which regularly sends forth missionaries. We do not send forth in proportion to our Catholic population as many missionaries as many another country. — Holland in that respect is ahead of all countries and ahead of us. — It is only still as a giver of money for foreign missions that we are foremost. But we do send out missionaries in scores and no country is increasing its Catholic missionaries at the rate we are ours.

Most of these missionaries belong to orders which are not of American foundation but which have become a part of our life : the Jesuits, the Franciscans, the Passionists, the Society of the Divine Word, the Oblates of Mary the Immaculate — to mention a few of them. — Through these orders many Americans have gone to India, China, Mesopotamia, the Solomon Islands. But most significant as witnessing to a sense of our land's obligation to Our Lady in handing on what we have received is a society known as the Catholic Foreign Mission Society of America. It was founded in the United States in 1912 and which began by sending forth four missionaries to China in 1918. It is called by a name which connects it with our past, and we hope with our future : Maryknoll.

The name Maryknoll incorporates the name of Our Lady into it, but even more than in name is the Society associated with her. It began in a manner after her heart, incongruously poor near to our greatest American show of riches, the City of New York. Even when it sent its first missionaries to China, it seemed to be pitifully un-important in comparison with the great doings that sur-rounded it, for the missionaries stepped west when the great crowd of American youth was still stepping east to the battlefields of Europe. And the size of the army going in the wrong direction was but four men, and who cared to look at them ?

The two founders of this Maryknoll were first Father James Anthony Walsh, later to become Bishop Walsh, and Father Thomas F. Price, later to become the first of the Maryknoll Fathers to die in the east. Both of these priests had since their days of preparation for the priest-hood dreamed of launching forth their country on a mis-sionary vocation. But they had begun at the beginning, far behind the starting line. Father Walsh as a student at St. John's Seminary, Boston, took up the habit of cor-responding with missionaries at the ends of the earth. Later he became Diocesan Director of the Society for the Propagation of the Faith at Boston, and in that office by a periodical, *The Field Afar*, he awakened a wide interest in just such missionaries as he had corresponded with. He established a kind of television by which peo-ple who thought only of their travels in Boston, New York and Philadelphia could catch a glimpse of a life to which it was easy to be blind — the life of the apostles of today to China, to India, to Africa. Father Price's en-thusiasm for missionaries led him on a different path : he became a missionary himself, not to China, but in a part of our country where Catholics are scarcest, North Caro-lina. He was of a more contemplative nature than Father

Walsh, and did a great deal of his particular work on his knees, before Our Lady of Lourdes, so much so that he came to be nicknamed "Father Bernadette" after the sainted French peasant girl who had seen Our Lady at Lourdes.

These two priests met in 1905 at the International Eucharistic Congress at Montreal. Seven years later they made a visit together to Europe. By then they had received the approval of the American bishops to the founding of a society for the training of missionary priests, and they were presenting the plan to the Holy Father. After they had received Rome's approval, one of them, Father Walsh, went traveling to study similar societies in Europe, and Father Price went to Lourdes, there to make a retreat. Their paths were ever different and their dispositions were different, yet they each supplemented the other. They were at one in their utter zeal for the new society which they were together bringing into being, and they were at one in taking it absolutely for granted that it was Our Lady's society. Even before they had a site for their college, even before they had any novices as students, they began to refer between themselves to their establishment as *Maryknoll*, as if it were some already existing place which they were discovering, not founding.

In 1911 they started their Maryknoll at a place called Hawthorne in New York State, about thirty miles from New York City — which was called Hawthorne because Nathaniel Hawthorne's daughter, turned a Catholic nun, was conducting there a cancer hospital. The two priests had a cottage there high enough to have the cold winds sweep across a valley to it, yet it was scarcely a knoll. It was certainly not *Maryknoll*.

Yet Mary of Bethlehem was there, and Hawthorne had its resemblance to inhospitable Bethlehem. It was a wonder that such a Bethlehem could have existed almost within sight of the highest peaks of New York's financial skyscrapers. There were in the Hawthorne community six students to learn, and three priests to teach, all living in a wooden house where the heating system worked only when the weather was hot, which was almost never, for 1911–12 was a winter perpetually below zero. In our land of modern improvements there was not even oil for lamps : candles had to be used. In our land of palatial plumbing there was not even water : the hand-pump would not even work by hand. At thirty miles from well-stored New York there was famine : Father Price had to beg Franciscan-like from house to house for bread. Father Walsh, going on fifty, had to cook without knowing how to cook. Father Lane, rheumatic, had to work the pump's arm without having his own arm that could move.

But spring came. A more appropriate site was at last found and bought for fifty thousand dollars. The price was majestic and the site too was majestic : it was situated at Ossining on the Hudson River, six miles from Hawthorne. It contained : "ninety-three acres of land, partly tilled, the rest wooded, on a splendid eminence, quite convenient to the metropolis, and within easy access of a considerable business center," so ran the realtor's account. There were even houses on the land. There was grandeur in this purchase, yet when the priests and students drove toward it, they looked like the tail-end of a bedraggled funeral procession, such as took place in the old days when motors were not yet used in funerals, for they drove to the Hudson in one of the last American hacks, seven of them breaking the springs of it, which were already broken, and the horse picking his way on three legs. But they arrived at their destination. And this time the knoll was Maryknoll.

"Hawthorne," wrote Father Walsh, "was our Bethlehem ; our Nazareth will be at Maryknoll, with the Queen of Apostles its protectress."

Maryknoll prospered. Its windows looked west to the East. Its young men went west to the East. They were entrusted first with 25,000 square miles of huge China in the province of Kwantung, in which lived eight million Chinese, and within those square miles in their first six years the Maryknoll priests converted a thousand adults, built a boys' school, a school for blind women, a school for catechists, then two other boys' schools, and finally a medical dispensary. It was merely a beginning, but it showed what Maryknoll could do in the future. And in recognition of what they could do, one-fifth of Korea was added to their field of operations, and finally, most touchingly, the district of Kongmoon which included the Island of Sancian where died the great missionary of missionaries, the great pioneer of them who itiated the modern missionary era — Saint Francis Xavier.

Within fifteen years from the trials at Hawthorne, Maryknoll had become more than a seed. Its three priests had grown to be seventy-eight. Counting missionaries, and student missionaries, and mission Sisters and mission Brothers, it was a corps of half a thousand. Its growth was significant in itself, but more significant in that it simply measured also a corresponding increase in vocations for foreign missions in a half-dozen other societies. The United States had ceased to be a missionary land in a passive sense ; in an active sense it was becoming one.

Of the Maryknollers the first to die in the field afar was Father Price. He had waited thirty years to become a missionary, and once he was what his heart desired, his heart was not asked to beat any more. His death was a consummation of his life. He became forever a missionary. Father Price may be some day hailed as a saint and canonized as a saint : Saint Bernadette. At any rate he will always be a legend. But he was not what missionary societies always accept with a sense that they have been divinely accredited : a martyr. He did not die a violent death at the hands of the heathen.

The first Maryknoll missioner to suffer a violent death for his faith in foreign lands was Father Gerard Donovan whose death came in 1938 in February. He was a native of Pittsburgh, Pennsylvania, born thus in the region where once stood in French days the Chapel of the Assumption of the Blessed Virgin of the Beautiful River. 1904 was the year of his birth, and 1931 was the year when he had his birth as a missionary, when he went to Manchukuo.

He was very American in his ingenuousness and eagerness. He had the youthfulness that Our Lady gives. In 1934 he passed Christmas at Hsin Pui and described the Midnight Mass : "The hushed, expectant Christians, the straw-thatched crib, the snowy white linens of the altar, and the red-cassocked slant-eyed altar boys, all these were a perfect setting for the Midnight Mass of my boyhood dreams. I would not trade it all for the most gorgeous Cathedral in Christendom." He also had an American sense of irony, of which Mark Twain is not the sole possessor. "Men-Kiang," he writes, "lies just a hundred miles northwest of Lin Kiang. A hundred miles would not be so far in the States, but my mule's speed is forty miles a day. Besides he is liable to burn out a bearing."

On one of his Manchukuoan trips he was made quite aware of the dangers he faced, and which his comrades faced, from bandits. One of these brigands, rifle in hand, arrested him and his slow mule one day, and brought him to a bandit leader. The leader looked on him and said, "Go your way." It was a surprise to receive such courtesy. "If bandits are all as courteous as those I have met so far," he wrote home, "there is little thrill in meeting them. If they are not — well, I leave that in God's hands."

His next encounter with bandits came two years later. He was not this time arrested on muleback. A man entered the sacristy of the church at Fushan on October 5th, and proceeded like an important intruder toward the sanctuary. Father Donovan was in the sanctuary at the time, praying during Benediction. Supposing the man was looking for some one and was simply unused to Catholic ceremonies, he led him back to the sacristy. After the Benediction was over, it was discovered that Father Donovan had disappeared, he and an altar boy, who had been in the sacristy also.

Two weeks later the altar boy returned and told how

the bandits had held them up, taken them to the hills. "We traveled all that night and for the next ten nights, sleeping in the hills during the day. Afterwards we remained in a sort of shelter, with roof, but no walls. We covered ourselves with grass at night, and we all suffered from the cold, but Father and I suffered from swollen feet as well." Such a life made Hawthorne seem a luxury.

Finally the bandits had let the boy, Francis Lien, go. There was no ransom to be received from him. They asked fourteen thousand for the freedom of Father Donovan. They kept him.

So back had trotted the boy to Fushan with his account of it all. He said : "Father was slim and tired when I last saw him, but in good spirits." After that there was no news of Father Donovan, and news was wanted by all, and especially by a brother of his, a priest in the United States, who had to go through November, December and January with no word. So he made a novena to Our Lady and to Father "Bernadette" Price, asking that he be relieved of the suspense. Let some news of his brother come. On the day of Our Lady of Lourdes a telegram came to the United States from China. A body had been discovered by a roadside near Haraijen, near Tung Hua. A telegram from the State Department at Washington to Maryknoll told the story of it :

"Ludden and Father Thomas Quirk of Catholic Church . . . report positive identification of the body discovered by the military authorities as that of Gerard Donovan. Difficult to determine exact time of death, but it is believed Father Donovan died at least one week before discovery of his remains. Emaciated condition of the scantily clad body indicated extreme hardship suffered during captivity ; body partially eaten by wolves. Military authorities state that there are no gunshot wounds and attribute death to strangulation." Then there came a sermon of eulogy at Maryknoll. The two founders of the society were now dead. It was a new superior who spoke. God, the "Divine Artist," he said, had presented Maryknoll with an example. God had spoken as it were to Maryknoll saying, "I give you a type — I give you a tradition."

When the Maryknoll superior used the word tradition he was thinking of the future. Maryknoll was to create from the death of this first of its slain priests a tradition for itself. But also the same death was the continuance of a tradition.

Father Donovan's death was a tradition carried on. He was Father Padilla living again, dying again, and the half a hundred martyred Franciscans of New Mexico and the eight martyred Spanish Jesuits of Virginia ; and the two Spanish Franciscans who went too far among the Apaches of Texas ; and Spanish Dominican Father Cancer of Florida, and all the other Spaniards ; and he was French Saint Isaac Jogues, martyred near Albany, New York, and French Father Foucault, the first martyr in French Louisiana, and the seven other martyrs that followed him, and the one slain Jesuit of Maine whose scalp was taken to Boston in the 1720's and paraded through the streets, and danced about as it was dangled from the pole which was the only May-pole that Calvinism with free conscience could dance about. He was but the repetition, told in the days of airplanes and radios, of an old tale, and of a tale that moved in the same slow and very human way.

That he should have died in China did not separate him from the martyrs that died in our country. To begin with, many of the early martyrs came to us wanting to go to China, and some of them thinking they were on the way there. But they and Father Donovan all had the same affair at heart, all similarly dedicated our country to Our Lady, the former by bringing the delight of Christians to our land, and the latter by keeping our land still in that delight by letting her diffuse it.

Thus the *Santa Maria* still has her consequences among us, and those consequences continue, but it is not my pen that writes them. It is the power that moves the stars and the other planets that will be their author.

INDEX

Abenaki Indians, 104, 105, 106, 135-6, 153, 234.
Adams, Henry, 126, 238-42.
Adams, John, 136, 139, 140.
Adams, Samuel, 135.
Agreda, Maria de, 31-2, 54.
Aiguillon, Duchesse d', 103.
Alabama, 69, 112.
Alexander VI, Pope, 5, 11.
Algonquins, Indian tribe, 71, 73.
Alleghanies, 98, 100, 101, 144, 190.
Allouez, Father, 112, 199.
"Angel Gabriel." See Orr.
Anza, Juan Bautista de, 29-30, 33.
Apache Indians, 30, 52.
Apalache Indians, 110.
Aquia Creek, 43.
Argall, Sir Samuel, 103.
Arizona, 6, 56 et seq.
Ark, The, 128, 139, 215.
Arkansas, 8, 69.
Arnold, Benedict, 137.
Arundel, Earl of, 122, 129, 141.
Avilés, Pedro. See Menéndez, Pedro Avilés de.
Ayllón, Lucas Vásquez de, 13-14, 15, 43.

Bahama Channel, 13, 39.
Baltimore, 151, 156-7, 187, 245.
Baltimore, Lord, 127, 139. See also Calvert.
Barat, Sophie, 220.
Bardstown, Kentucky, 166.
Barron, Bishop Edward, 246.
Beecher, Rev. Lyman, 183, 223.
Benavides, Alonzo, Spanish chronicler, 52.
Benton, Thomas H., 203.
Berkeley, William, governor of Virginia, 131.
Bernard, St., 1-2.

Blanchet, Francis Norbert, bishop of Oregon, 245.
Bohemia Manor, Maryland, 216.
Bolton, Herbert, historian, 28.
Boone, Daniel, 8.
Borgia, St. Francis, 40-1.
Boston, 125, 151-3, 166, 178, 179, 223.
Braddock, General Edward, 101, 144.
Brazil, 5.
Breckenridge, Rev. R. J., 182.
British Columbia, 202.
Brosius, F. X., 157, 161, 218.
Brulé, Etienne, 72 et seq., 75.
Bruté de Rémur, Simon William Gabriel, bishop of Vincennes, 230.
Bruyas, Father, 105.
Bucarelli, Viceroy, 58.

Cabeza de Vaca, Alvar Núñez, Spanish explorer, 15-20, 25, 32.
Cabot, John, Italian navigator, 120.
Cabrillo, Estévan, Spanish explorer, 20-1, 34.
Cabrini, Mother Frances Xavier, 229.
California, 6, 20, 29, 57 et seq.
Calvert, Cecil, 129.
Calvert, George, 127 et seq., 132.
Calvert, Leonard, 129.
Calvinists, 122 et seq., 240.
Canary Islands, 55.
Cancer, Father Luis, 42, 255.
Cannon Ball River, 205.
Cape Cod, 70.
Capuchins, 104, 105, 108.
Cardeñas, Spanish explorer, 26.
Carmelites, 150.
Carolinas, 100.
Carroll, Daniel, 139, 140, 149.